A GUIDE TO READING SHAKESPEARE'S *OTHELLO*

A GUIDE TO READING
SHAKESPEARE'S *OTHELLO*

MARIA FRANZISKA FAHEY

Maria Franziska Fahey is the author of *Metaphor and Shakespearean Drama: Unchaste Signification*, which was shortlisted for the 2012 Shakespeare's Globe Book Award. She is a member of the faculty at Friends Seminary, where she has taught English for more than twenty-five years.

Copyright © 2017 by Maria Franziska Fahey

All rights reserved.

Except for the use of brief quotations in a book review, no part of this book may be reproduced in any form by any electronic or mechanical means without the express written permission of the author.

First Printing, 2017
Second Printing, 2021, contains corrections and minor revisions of the text.
Third Printing, 2022, contains corrections and minor revisions of the text.

ISBN-13: 978-0692926444

ISBN-10: 0692926445

Accabonac Press
61 Jane Street, Suite 17C, New York, NY 10014

Cover illustration and design by Lauren Simkin Berke

CONTENTS

Preface vii
    On the Pleasures & Challenges of Reading Shakespeare's Dramatic Language vii
    Using This Guide ix
    Hearing & Seeing Performances ix

Questions to Consider as You Read *Othello* 1
    Larger Questions 1
    Patterns of Figurative Language 3
    Act 1, Scene 1 4
    Act 1, Scene 2 12
    Act 1, Scene 3 15
    Act 2, Scene 1 26
    Act 2, Scene 2 35
    Act 2, Scene 3 36
    Act 3, Scene 1 43
    Act 3, Scene 2 45
    Act 3, Scene 3 46
    Act 3, Scene 4 58
    Act 4, Scene 1 63
    Act 4, Scene 2 68
    Act 4, Scene 3 73
    Act 5, Scene 1 75
    Act 5, Scene 2 78

Appendices 86
    1. Listening for Meter—An Introduction 86
    2. Reading Figurative Language—An Introduction to Metaphor, Simile, Metonymy, &
    Synecdoche 90
    3. On How an Edition of *Othello* Is Made 98

Acknowledgments 100

PREFACE

On the Pleasures & Challenges of Reading Shakespeare's Dramatic Language

Reading Shakespeare's plays can be immensely pleasurable, but doing so is no easy task. Whereas we now get a great deal of our information through visual images, including photographs and film, in Shakespeare's day most information came through spoken language. Part of the fun, and also the challenge, of reading a Shakespeare play is having to transform language into visual images for ourselves.

Indeed, Shakespeare was aware of the demands he was making of his audiences. In the Prologue to his play *The Life of Henry the Fifth*, the Chorus admits that it cannot bring King Henry himself or "the vasty fields of France" into the theater and so asks the members of the audience to let the play work on their "imaginary forces" (*Henry V* Pro. 12, 18). The Chorus goes on to suggest, "Think, when we talk of horses, that you see them, / Printing their proud hoofs i'th' receiving earth" (Pro. 26-7).

A Shakespeare play is largely "talk"—a series of conversations among a cast of characters. However, the talk of a Shakespeare play is often more difficult to understand than ordinary speech because it has been crafted to bring a whole world before our eyes. The series of questions in this guide is designed to help you listen carefully, scene-by-scene, to what the characters say so that you can use your "imaginary forces" to see the world of *Othello* for yourself. As you read the play's language and begin to envision its world, it will be helpful to remain aware of how the language spoken by characters in the play is different from that of ordinary speech. Here are a few of these differences:

Vocabulary. Written over 400 years ago, the plays are known for their unusually large vocabularies, including many words that were, at the time, new to the English language—some probably invented by Shakespeare himself. Almost all readers find the rich vocabulary of a Shakespeare play challenging to understand even as they come to enjoy the subtle and abundant connotations of the words Shakespeare chose. Furthermore, twenty-first century readers will find that the meanings of some words have changed since Shakespeare's day and that other words, rarely spoken now, have become obsolete. For instance, the word *napkin* in Othello's complaint, "Your napkin is too little" (*Othello* 3.3.287) refers to Desdemona's handkerchief. And the word *doubt* can mean "suspect," as it does in Othello's assertion, "I'll see before I doubt; when I doubt, prove" (3.3.191). Be sure to consult the notes in your copy of the play and to keep a good dictionary at hand, one that provides older meanings of words. (Check your library's print or online version of *The Oxford English Dictionary*—the *OED*—which is the most comprehensive English dictionary.)

But don't feel obligated to look up every word when first reading a play. You can understand a great deal about unfamiliar words from their context. Consider, for instance, the context of the word *clogs* in Brabantio's remark to his daughter, Desdemona, who recently has eloped:

> I am glad at soul I have no other child,
> For thy escape would teach me tyranny,
> To hang clogs on them. (1.3.197-9)

You might not know what *clog* means here. But you can figure out that if Brabantio says that his daughter's escaping would teach him to "hang clogs" on any other child he had, then a clog must be a device that would restrain someone by making it hard to move. (The *Oxford English Dictionary* defines *clog* as "A block or heavy piece of wood attached to the leg or neck of a man or beast to impede motion or prevent escape" (*OED* 2a).)

Poetic Language. The conversations in a Shakespeare play are no ordinary conversations: they were crafted by a poet-playwright who used sound, rhythm, and imagery to convey his meanings. Consider the lines spoken by Lodovico at the end of the play's final scene:

> Myself will straight aboard, and to the state
> This heavy act with heavy heart relate. (5.2.369-70)

In ordinary speech, someone would likely say, "I will go straight aboard and, with heavy heart, relate this heavy act to the state." But Shakespeare's word choice ("Myself" instead of "I," for instance) and his word order allow the lines to be in perfect iambic pentameter and to rhyme ("state" with "relate"). This couplet adds a sense of finality at the end of *Othello*'s chaotic final scene. *(For an explanation of* iambic pentameter *and* couplet, *see appendix 1, pages 86-87.)*

Descriptions that Provide Context. Although Shakespeare's theater included costumes and some props, it did not include sets or lighting. (The use of electricity was centuries away, and plays were performed at The Globe, an open-air theater, in the mid-afternoon.) Audiences would have to glean important context from the characters' speeches. For instance, in act 2, scene 1 of *Othello*, we hear about a storm at sea that Montano observes from land. Describing the wind on land, Montano wonders what "ribs of oak" (of a wooden ship) could hold together as the "mountains" (big waves) "melt on" (wash over) them:

> Montano   Methinks the wind hath spoke aloud at land,
> A fuller blast ne'er shook our battlements.
> If it hath ruffianed so upon the sea,
> What ribs of oak, when mountains melt on them,
> Can hold the mortise? (2.1.5-9)

Nowadays such images and sounds of a storm at sea could be shown to a theater audience through lighting design, sets, and special effects. Thus, contemporary playwrights usually don't write such descriptions into characters' speeches, and contemporary audiences don't have to decipher and picture them.

Implied Action. Unlike stories or novels, most plays don't have a narrator who tells us what characters are doing as they speak to each other. Playwrights can indicate specific actions with stage directions, but Shakespeare's plays have relatively few. Instead, the dialogue itself gives clues about characters' actions. Consider the scene where Desdemona tries to persuade Othello that she is innocent. At one point, she asks Othello:

> Desdemona   Alas, why gnaw you so your nether lip?
> Some bloody passion shakes your very frame. (5.2.43-4)

Desdemona's lines let us see Othello's physical state—he shakes and gnaws his lower ("nether") lip—and provide direction to the actor playing *Othello*. Imagining the world of a Shakespeare play depends, in part, on listening for clues to characters' actions. Try acting out a scene with some friends: doing so will help you become attentive to such clues.

Learning to see the world of a Shakespeare play by reading or hearing its language takes some work and some patience. However, paying close attention to the play's language will give you access to the most interesting, complicated, and surprising aspects of the plays. As the Prologue to *The Life of Henry the Fifth* shows, Shakespeare invited and relied on his audiences to envision the worlds of his plays, and he gave us incomparable language from which to do so. There are always many ways to imagine a phrase, line, or scene, but it's important to start with accurate observations of the play's language.

Using This Guide

The series of questions for each scene will help you to observe the sometimes complex and dense language accurately and to puzzle through the characters' conversations. Before trying to answer the questions for a particular scene, read through the entire scene aloud. Or, better yet, gather some friends, take parts, and read the scene aloud together. Don't be shy: you might mispronounce a word or need to read some lines slowly, but you will have a much better chance of understanding the lines when you read them aloud—and you likely will have more fun. Then, read through the scene again slowly, answering the questions as you go. If you don't fully understand a question, quote the phrase or line that you suspect contains the clues for its answer. Once you reach the scene's end, return to those questions to see if you have been able to figure out anything further.

Some of the questions use terms and refer to methods with which you may not be familiar: they may ask you to observe and analyze "meter" or "figurative language," especially "metaphor." Don't worry if you are not familiar with these terms or if you never have "scanned a line of verse" or "sorted a metaphor's tenor and vehicle": you will find the necessary background information and sample analyses in the appendices. Appendix 1, "Listening for Meter," explains how to identify the basic rhythms of Shakespeare's poetry; appendix 2, "Reading Figurative Language," explains how to identify and analyze figures of speech; and appendix 3, "On How an Edition of *Othello* Is Made," explains how the copy of *Othello* you are reading is derived from the earliest texts of the play and lets you know what kinds of additions and changes an editor may have made in preparing the play for publication. You may find it helpful to read through these appendices before you begin to answer the questions. Or you may consult them when you arrive at a question that requires your knowledge of the information they provide. All of the information in the appendices aims to help you to understand and envision the play for yourself.

Quotations in this guide are taken from the edition of *Othello* edited by Burton Raffel and published by Yale University Press in 2005. Following standard scholarly practice, quotations are followed by a citation that indicates the act, scene, and lines from which a passage is quoted. So, for instance, "(3.1.6-7)" refers to act 3, scene 1, lines 6-7. If you are reading a different edition of the play, your line numbers may be slightly different. *(See appendix 3, "On How an Edition of* Othello *Is Made," for an explanation of how the differences in editions come about.)*

Hearing & Seeing Performances

If, after reading aloud by yourself and with friends, you continue to have trouble getting the gist of what the characters are saying to each other, try to locate a good audio recording of the play, one that has been recorded by a cast of experienced Shakespearean actors. (Many libraries have them available.) Read along as you listen to the audio recording of the scene you are working on. Hearing trained actors deliver the characters' lines will likely help you understand much of what the characters are saying. Keep in mind that the way an actor speaks a line depends on that actor's interpretation of it and that you might have another interpretation.

After reading the play, you might enjoy seeing a performance of it. Check to see if there is a live performance at a nearby theater, or borrow a film of the play from your library. If you wait to see a performance until after reading the play, you will be able to compare the way you have imagined the play-world to the way a particular director has. If you see the performance before you've read the play, be aware, as you read, that the particular director's vision of the play is not the only possibility: one good way to do so is to see two, or more, performances or films.

There are many books and websites that publish summaries and analyses of Shakespeare's plays. Be wary. Don't accept another reader's vision of the play too easily: your own careful reading and imagining might lead you to a far more interesting one!

QUESTIONS TO CONSIDER AS YOU READ *OTHELLO*

Larger Questions

As you answer the questions for each scene, you often will be prompted to think about the topics listed below. (Some will overlap.) If you are particularly interested in one of these topics, you might find it helpful to keep track of what various characters say about it by marking relevant passages in your text or by keeping a list of relevant passages in a notebook. When you have finished reading the play, you then will be ready to consider the collection of passages you have gathered and to ask yourself what the play as a whole might be suggesting about the topic. This kind of work is one way to prepare to write an essay about *Othello*.

1. **Honesty.** Who calls whom *honest*? What is the effect of the repetition of the word? Who calls whom *false*? What, in the end, does the play suggest about honesty? Keep in mind that in Shakespeare's day *honest* had a wider range of meanings than now. Here are some of the definitions listed in the *Oxford English Dictionary*:

    - "holding a position of honour, respectable" (2a), "truthful, trustworthy" (4b), "free from guile, straightforward, frank" (4d);
    - "virtuous" (3a), "Esp. of a woman: virtuous as regards sexual morality, chaste" (3b); and
    - "as a general epithet of appreciation or praise, esp. as used in a patronizing way to or of an inferior" (2b).

2. **Eyes & Sight.** What do characters say about eyes and seeing? What is the relation between seeing and knowing?

3. **Signs, Forms, Visages, Flags, & Proof.** When do characters refer to something they see as a *sign*? How do they interpret these signs? What does the play suggest about the relation between signs and truth?

4. **Doubting & Knowing.** What makes characters doubt or suspect others or themselves? What makes them think they know something or someone?

5. **Voice, Speech, Stories, & Tales.** What do characters say about speech and stories? Who is allowed to speak in public? Who must ask permission to speak? Who tells stories? What is their effect?

6. **Ears & Hearing.** What do characters say about ears? About the effect of hearing news or a story?

7. **Thoughts, Feelings, & Acts.** What can characters tell about what another character is thinking or feeling from how they act or what they say?

8. **Passion (Heart, Blood, Stomach) & Reason (Cause).** When are characters motivated by passion? When by reason? What does the play suggest about the powers and dangers of each?

9. **Love & Desire.** What do characters say about love? What about desire?

10. **Witchcraft, Charms, Spells & Minerals.** Who is said to use witchcraft? What other than witchcraft is said to be enchanting or beguiling?

11. **Identity.** How are people identified by others? How do they identify themselves? Which identities are accompanied by privileges or allow social mobility? Which identities bring disadvantages or restrict social mobility? Are some identities accompanied by certain privileges and certain disadvantages? How do identities overlap? Consider:

    - **city, country, or region** (Venetian, Florentine, Veronesa, Ottomite, Turkish, Cypriate, Barbarian (of Barbary), Mauratanian);
    - **gender**;
    - **age**;
    - **appearance** (skin color, beauty);
    - **wealth** (land, money, jewels);
    - **family role** (wife, daughter, father, husband); and
    - **social role or rank** (duke, general, lieutenant, ancient, servant, maid).

12. **Marriage, Husbands, & Wives.** What do characters say about what it means to be a husband or a wife? What do they say about the nature of marriage?

13. **Strangers.** Who and what is considered foreign or strange? How is foreignness characterized? Who are the Venetians in the play? How is Venice characterized?

14. **Color, Complexion, Black, & White.** What do people say about skin color? When is color—especially black and white or fair—spoken of literally? When figuratively? What are characters' attitudes toward color?

15. **Money, Purses, Crusadoes, Riches, Jewels, & Prizes.** What do people say about various forms of wealth? Who has money? How do differences in wealth affect relationships?

16. **The Domestic World & the World Outside.** How do characters talk about what is appropriate for home (house, chambers) and for the outside world (state, field)? How is gender associated with each world? How do characters imagine the relation between home and state?

17. **Suitors, Suits, Mediators, & Go-betweens.** How do characters pursue their goals, their *suits*? When do characters use a "go-between" or "mediator" instead of speaking directly to another? What are the effects of involving a third party? How do characters use others to help them achieve what they desire?

18. **Reputation, Name, Honor, & Slander.** What do characters say about reputation? How are characters' reputations ruined? How are they restored?

19. **Justice & Revenge.** What motivates characters to pursue justice? What motivates revenge?

20. **Fate, Fortune, & Destiny.** What do characters say about destiny? About God and the gods?

Patterns of Figurative Language

Questions for each scene also will prompt you to notice and analyze figurative language. *(See appendix 1 for an introduction to figurative language.)* Sometimes one instance of figurative language echoes figurative language from other scenes in the play. These patterns of figurative language are an important part of how the play is structured and delivers its meanings. You might find it helpful to keep track of repeating figures by marking instances of them in your text or by keeping a list in a notebook. When you have finished reading the play, you then will be ready to ask yourself what the pattern suggests or means. In *Othello*, be on the lookout for figures of:

1. Storms & Other Natural Phenomena
2. Ships, Sailing, & the Sea
3. Animals & Insects
4. Monsters & Cuckolds
5. Prostitutes (whores, strumpets, callats, minxes)
6. Hunger & Eating (stomach, devour, eat, belch, englut, swallow)
7. Poison, Pestilence, Plague, & Medicine
8. Hunting (taming, checking, seeling)
9. Birth & Womb (conceive, get, beget, engender)
10. Darkness & Light
11. Bondage & Slavery
12. Weaving, Webs, & Spinning
13. Pageants & Plays
14. Music, Harmony, & Discord

ACT 1, SCENE 1

As the play begins, Roderigo and Iago are in the middle of a conversation. If you're reading the play for the first time, it will be impossible to follow all they are talking about. As you continue reading and hear more of their conversation, more will become clear. But even by the scene's end, there's much you will not yet have heard, including the name of "the Moor"[1] (Othello) or of Brabantio's daughter (Desdemona).

Read through the entire scene, noting all clues about the subject and tone of Roderigo and Iago's conversation and about what they go on to do at the house of Signior Brabantio. Also note references that you don't understand. Then, once you reach the scene's end, begin again, answering the questions below as you reread.

1. How did you feel as you struggled to understand Roderigo and Iago's opening conversation—and other confusing events in act 1, scene 1? What is the mood at the start of *Othello*?

2. Before learning that his daughter has eloped, Brabantio tells Roderigo, "My daughter is not for thee" (1.1.96). What is Roderigo's interest in Brabantio's daughter? What has been Brabantio's opinion of Roderigo?

3. Now that you've read the entire scene, what do you understand about why Roderigo is upset with Iago? To what does *this* refer in "shouldst know of this" (1.1.3)? To whom does *him* refer in "Thou told'st me / Thou didst hold him in thy hate" (1.1.5-6)?

4. Quote and explain what Roderigo says to Iago about his purse (1.1.2-3). What does this comment suggest about their relationship?

---

[1] The *Oxford English Dictionary* gives the following definition for *Moor*: "originally: a native or inhabitant of ancient Mauretania, a region of North Africa corresponding to parts of present-day Morocco and Algeria. Later usually: a member of a Muslim people of mixed Berber and Arab descent inhabiting north-western Africa" (*OED* 1).

5. Notice that Iago responds to Roderigo's complaint ("I take it much unkindly" (1.1.1)) with the news that Michael Cassio has been made lieutenant while he, Iago, has been made "his Moorship's ancient" (1.1.30-1). (An *ancient*, a lower rank than lieutenant, is responsible for carrying the officer's ensign or banner.) As you look again at what Iago says about the recently appointed lieutenant, keep in mind that Iago presents this news in response to Roderigo's concern (1.1.6-38):

   a. For what did Iago employ "mediators" (1.1.14)?

   b. Where is Michael Cassio from?

   c. What does Iago mean when he calls Cassio "a great arithmetician" (1.1.17)? With what tone might Iago say this?

   d. What evidence does Iago present that Cassio is "Mere prattle, without practice" (1.1.24)? (*Prattle* is "foolish, inconsequential, or incomprehensible talk" (*OED* 1).) What "practice" does Iago claim Cassio lacks that he himself has?

   e. Iago complains that he "must be belee'd and calmed" by Cassio (1.1.28). *Be-lee'd* means, "To get (a ship) into such a position that the wind is intercepted from her" (*OED* 1); *calmed*, which can mean "Detained by a calm" (*OED* b). As what does Iago imagine himself here? *(For an analysis of this metaphor, see appendix 2, page 93.)*

   f. How, according to Iago, does "preferment"—promotion—happen (1.1.34)? Quote and explain Iago's phrase.

   g. Iago concludes, "be judge yourself / Whether I in any just term am affined / To love the Moor" (1.1.36-8). Of what is Iago trying to convince Roderigo by telling this story about not having been promoted?

6. Roderigo insists, "I would not follow him, then" (1.1.38). What does Roderigo suggest about Iago's remaining in the service of the Moor? What does Roderigo imply about the relation between what one feels or thinks and how one acts?

7. Explain Iago's assertion: "I follow him to serve my turn upon him" (1.1.40).

8. Summarize Iago's description of the two ways of serving one's master—"Many a duteous and knee-crooking knave" and "Others [. . .] trimmed in forms and visages of duty" (1.1.43-52). Which type of servant does Iago profess he is?

9. Iago concludes, "In following him, I follow but myself" (1.1.56) and explains:

    > For when my outward action doth demonstrate
    > The native act and figure of my heart
    > In complement extern, 'tis not long after
    > But I will wear my heart upon my sleeve
    > For daws to peck at. (1.1.59-63)

    a. What reason does Iago give for not allowing his "outward action" to show the "native act and figure" of his heart? (*Native* here means "connected with something by nature" (*OED* 1a).) What does Iago claim would happen to his heart if he did so?

    b. Do you think Iago has a point? Have you ever not demonstrated what was in your heart for fear of injury?

10. What might Iago mean when he says, "I am not what I am" (1.1.63)? How does this assertion compare to "I am not what I *seem*"?

11. EXTRA OPPORTUNITY. Read (or reread) the story in the Bible's Book of Exodus where God tells Moses, "I AM That I Am" (Exodus 3:14). How does Iago vary what God says? To what effect?

12. Notice that Iago's explanation (that he will hide what is naturally in his heart) seems to satisfy, or at least to distract, Roderigo, who stops complaining about what Iago has done to him and turns his attention to "the Moor." What advice would you give Roderigo about Iago?

13. To what or whom does Roderigo refer with the expression "thick-lips" (1.1.64)? Explain how "thick-lips" is an example of synecdoche. *(For an explanation of synecdoche, see appendix 2, page 97.)* How does this term work as an insult?

14. What does Iago incite Roderigo to do? Whose "delight" does Iago urge Roderigo to "poison" (1.1.66)? What simile does Iago use to describe the manner in which Roderigo should yell (1.1.74-75)?

15. What do we learn about the scene's setting (including the time) and about Brabantio's experience of Roderigo and Iago's arrival at his house? Jump ahead to the exchange below which contains key clues.

    Roderigo   Most reverend signior, do you know my voice?
    Brabantio   Not I. What are you?
    Roderigo   My name is Roderigo. (1.1.91-2)

    How would you stage this scene? (Under what conditions would it make sense for Roderigo to ask, "do you know my *voice*"?) How would you direct the actor playing Brabantio?

16. Now go back and consider how Iago, who never identifies himself to Brabantio, alarms him: "Thieves, thieves, thieves! / Look to your house, your daughter, and your bags! / Thieves, thieves!" (1.1.77-9). What does Iago's sequence—house, daughter, bags—suggest about a father's relationship to his daughter? What is the effect of Iago's repetition of the word "thieves"?

17. Iago then proclaims, "you have lost half your soul" (1.1.85). What does he now suggest about a father's relationship to his daughter?

18. Consider Iago's calling out to Brabantio:

    Even now, now, very now, an old black ram
    Is tupping your white ewe. (1.1.86-7)

    What is the effect of these animal metaphors of Othello and Desdemona on the night they elope? (A *ram* is an adult male sheep; a *ewe* is a female sheep; to *tup*, said of a ram, means to copulate (have sex with) a ewe.) What is the effect of the repetition of "now"?

19. Iago continues to warn Brabantio, "Arise [. . .] Or else the devil will make a grandsire out of you" (1.1.87-90). What does Iago emphasize by warning Brabantio that he will be made a "grandsire" (grandfather) by "the devil," Othello? What does Iago imply would be a father's concern about his daughter's marriage partner?

20. Why had Brabantio "charged [Roderigo] not to haunt about [his] doors" (1.1.94)?

21. "This is Venice, / My house is not a grange" (1.1.104-5). (A *grange* is a barn or a house with a farm (*OED* 1, 2)). What does Brabantio imply about Venice? About the city compared to the country?

22. Reread 1.1.107-115 ("Zounds, sir [. . .] with two backs"). What further metaphors and images does Iago use to alarm Brabantio?

23. What "answer" does Roderigo give to Brabantio (1.118-38)? Summarize it.

24. Roderigo calls Othello "a lascivious Moor" (1.1.124) and "an extravagant and wheeling stranger" (1.1.134). What does Roderigo emphasize about Othello? How do his references to Othello compare to Iago's? (*Lascivious* means "inclined to lust" (*OED* 1); *extravagant* can mean "That wanders out of bounds; straying, roaming, vagrant" (*OED* 1).)

25. Brabantio remarks, "This accident is not unlike my dream, / Belief of it oppresses me already" (1.1.140-1). (Here *accident* means "An occurrence, event" (*OED* 5b).) How surprised is Brabantio that his daughter has eloped? How does he feel about her having done so?

26. What explanation does Iago give Roderigo for leaving before Brabantio comes out of his house (1.1.142-157)?

    a. For what "business" does the state need Othello (1.1.151)?

    b. What are the possible meanings of *sign*? "Though I do hate him as I do hell's pains / Yet for the necessity of present life, / I must show out a flag and sign of love, / Which is indeed but sign" (1.1.152-5). (Remember that Iago is Othello's *ancient*, his flag bearer.)

27. Iago says he will be at "the Sagittary," where Roderigo "shall surely find" Othello (1.1.155-6). What does Iago's knowledge of Othello's whereabouts on the night he has eloped indicate about Othello's relationship with Iago?

28. Brabantio announces, "Fathers, from hence trust not your daughters' minds / By what you see them act" (1.1.168-9). What does Brabantio seem to believe his daughter's actions reveal about all daughters? What do you think about his logic?

29. What does Brabantio suggest is a possible reason that his daughter eloped when he asks, "Is there not charms / By which the property of youth and maidhood / May be abused" (1.1.169-71)? (*Abused* can mean "deceived.") Who, does Brabantio imply, might have used such charms?

30. How does Brabantio feel now about Roderigo as a suitor? ("O, would you had had her!" (1.1.173).) How do you account for Brabantio's change of attitude toward Roderigo? (*Would* here means "I wish.")

ACT 1, SCENE 2

1. About whom is Iago speaking when he says, "I had thought to have yerked him here, under the ribs" (1.2.5)?

2. How does what Iago tells Othello about what happened at Brabantio's house differ from what you witnessed?

3. Who is the "Magnifico" (1.2.11)? About what does Iago warn Othello (1.2.11-16)?

4. How does Othello respond to Iago's news about Brabantio? What does Othello mean when he says that his services shall "out-tongue" Brabantio's complaints" (1.2.17-18)? What does this response show about Othello?

5. What does Othello offer as evidence that he loves Desdemona (1.2.24-7)? Quote and explain the key phrase.

6. Iago says that the men approaching with lights are Brabantio ("the raisèd father") and his friends (1.2.28). On what basis does Othello reject Iago's advice to go inside (1.2.30-1)? What does Iago imply will happen if Othello remains where he is?

7. In fact, the men approaching are the Duke's servants and Othello's new lieutenant, Cassio, who tells Othello that the Duke "requires" his "haste—post-haste—appearance" (1.2.36). Why is the Duke urgently calling for Othello in the middle of the night?

8. Iago lets Cassio know that Othello has just been married by saying, "Faith, he tonight hath boarded a land carack. / If it prove lawful prize, he's made forever" (1.2.49-50). (A *carack* is "A large ship [. . .] such as those formerly used by the Portuguese in trading with the East Indies; a galleon (*OED*).) Analyze the metaphor:

vehicle	:	tenor
_____	:	he (Othello)
boarded	:	_____
carack	:	_____
prize	:	_____

   What does this metaphor indicate about Iago's attitude toward marriage?

9. Cassio responds, "I do not understand," and asks, married "To who?" (1.2.51). Give two or three reasons Cassio might respond this way to Iago's announcing Othello's marriage.

10. How does Othello treat Brabantio? Start by quoting one or two key phrases from which you derive your answer.

11. What reasons does Brabantio give for accusing Othello of using charms, magic, and drugs on his daughter. Quote and explain two key phrases.

12. How does Othello respond to Brabantio's accusation? What does his response show about Othello?

13. Quote the couplet at the end of the scene (1.2.97-98). With what argument does Brabantio demand that his daughter's marriage to Othello be stopped? What does he suggest will happen in the state of Venice if the marriage is allowed?

ACT 1, SCENE 3

1. Reread 1.3.1-47 ("There is no composition [. . .] the valiant Moor"). What inconsistent reports are the Duke and Senators discussing? What do all the reports nonetheless confirm? Briefly explain the senators' discussion of the Turks ("the Ottomites"), Rhodes, and Cyprus. (*Ottomites* is another name for the Ottomans or Turks.)

2. EXTRA RESEARCH OPPORTUNITY. Find a seventeenth-century map in a history book or on the internet; notice the boundaries of the Ottoman Empire; and make a quick sketch of a map showing Venice, Turkey, Rhodes, Cyprus, and Mauritania.

3. To what does Senator 1 refer when he says, "'Tis a pageant / To keep us in false gaze" (1.3.18-19)? Memorize this sentence.

4. How does the Duke address Othello? Fill in the blank: "_____ Othello" (1.3.48).

5. Sketch Brabantio's description of his grief. ("*Englut* means "to gulp down" (*OED* 1).)

   > For my particular grief
   > Is of so floodgate and o'erbearing nature
   > That it engluts and swallows other sorrows,
   > And it is still itself. (1.3.55-8)

6. What does the Duke and Senators' question "Dead?" indicate about how Brabantio must be acting (1.3.59)? How would you direct an actor to perform Brabantio in this scene?

7. What reason does Brabantio give for his assertion that witchcraft was used on his daughter (1.3.61-5)?

8. What does the Duke say will happen to whoever "Hath thus beguiled [Brabantio's] daughter of herself" (1.3.66-71)?

9. Reread Othello's response (1.3.77-95) to the Duke's asking what he can say in response to Brabantio's accusation (1.3.75):

   a. What does Othello say is the "extent" of his "offending" (1.3.81-2)?

   b. What explanation does Othello give for his assertion, "Rude am I in my speech, / And little blessed with the soft phrase of peace" (1.3.82-3)? (*Rude* can mean "violent, harsh" (*OED* 2), "unskilled, uneducated" (*OED* 3), and "uncultured, uncivilized" (*OED* 4).)

   c. What adjectives does Othello use to describe the kind of tale he will deliver (1.3.91)? Quote them:

   "I will a _____ _____ tale deliver."

   d. What does he imply other kinds of tales can be?

10. What are Desdemona's characteristics, according to her father, that make him vouch that she was won "with some mixtures powerful o'er the blood" (1.3.95-107)?

11. Note the Duke's response and fill in the blank: "To vouch this is no _____" (1.3.107). (*Vouch* here means "To allege, assert, affirm or declare" (*OED* 4).)

12. How does Othello respond to the First Senator's request that he speak (1.3.115-21)? What does Othello's response show about how he regards Desdemona?

13. While they go to fetch Desdemona, Othello tells his story (1.3.128-70). Reread Othello's speech and answer the following according to Othello:

    a. How did Desdemona and Othello meet?

    b. What kinds of stories would Othello tell Brabantio about his past? Before coming to Venice, where had Othello been? What had he done? What had happened to him? Quote a few key phrases.

    c. Othello says that Desdemona would "with haste dispatch" the "house affairs" and, "with a greedy ear / Devour up my discourse" (1.3.147-50). Analyze this metaphor. (Here *discourse* means "A narrative or account of a particular subject" (*OED* 3b).)

vehicle	:	tenor
greedy	:	_____
_____	:	ear
devour	:	_____
_____	:	discourse

    d. How did Othello "beguile" Desdemona "of her tears" (1.3.156)? (*Beguile* can mean "to cheat out of" (*OED* 2).)

    e. For what did Desdemona give Othello kisses?

    f. What did Desdemona tell Othello would "woo" her (1.3.166)? (*Woo* means "To solicit or sue a woman in love; to court" (*OED* 1a).)

    g. How did Othello understand this "hint" (1.3.166)?

h. Fill in the blanks: "She loved me for _____, / And I loved her that _____" (1.3.167-8).

i. What kind of "witchcraft" does Othello admit to having used?

j. Do you agree with Othello's earlier assertion that he is "rude" in his speech (1.3.82)? How would you characterize Othello's speech?

14. How does the Duke respond to Othello's account? Complete the sentence: "I think this tale would _____" (1.3.171).

15. How does Desdemona respond to her father's question, "Do you perceive in all this noble company / Where most you owe obedience" (1.3.179-80)?

16. What would prompt Brabantio to say, "I had rather to adopt a child than get it" (1.3.192)? (*Get*, short for *beget*, means "to bring (a child) into existence by the process of reproduction" (*OED* 2a).) What does Brabantio imply about being a biological father?

17. Why is Brabantio "glad at soul" he has "no other child" (1.3.197)?

18. Read aloud the Duke's speech at 1.3.203-10 ("When remedies are past [. . .] bootless grief"). What does the Duke attempt to accomplish? What is the effect of his speaking in couplets? *(For an explanation of* couplet, *see appendix 1, page 86.)*

19. Paraphrase the Duke's last couplet: "The robbed that smiles steals something from the thief. / He robs himself that spends a bootless grief" (1.3.209-10). (*Bootless* means "incurable, remediless" (*OED* 2).)

20. Read aloud Brabantio's response (1.3.211-20). How does he reply? What is the effect of Brabantio's speaking his response in couplets?

21. Paraphrase Brabantio's last couplet: "But words are words: I never yet did hear / That the bruisèd heart was piercèd through the ear" (1.3.219-20). (To pierce can mean "To affect keenly or deeply with emotion" (*OED* 5).)

22. How does Othello respond to the Duke's command that he "slubber the gloss of [his] new fortunes" with the "more stubborn and boisterous expedition" to Cyprus (1.3.226-9)? What is Othello's concern about leaving for war now that he is married (1.3.230-40)?

23. How does Desdemona support her request to go with Othello? Be sure to explain: "I saw Othello's visage in his mind, / And to his honors and his valiant parts / Did I my soul and fortunes consecrate" (1.3.253-5). (*Visage* means "face"; consecrate means "To set apart as sacred to the Deity" (*OED* 1).)

24. What does Othello assure the Duke is *not* the reason he wants the Duke to grant Desdemona's request (1.3.261-6)? What are "the young affects" that he claims are "defunct" in him (1.3.264-5)?

25. What does he assure the Duke will *not* be an effect of Desdemona's being with him (1.3.267-9)?

26. Consider Othello's speech:

    > No, when light-winged toys
    > Of feathered Cupid seel with wanton dullness
    > My speculative and officed instruments,
    > That my disports corrupt and taint my business
    > Let housewives make a skillet of my helm. (1.3.269-73)

    How does Othello imagine the effects of Cupid (god of erotic love) on a warrior? What are his "speculative and officed instruments"? (*Seel* means "to make blind" (*OED* 2); *wanton* means "undisciplined" (*OED* 1); a *skillet* is metal cooking pot (*OED* 1); and *helm* here means "helmet" (*OED* 1).)

27. To whose "conveyance" does Othello "assign [his] wife" (1.3.285-6)?

28. Explain the Duke's parting couplet to Brabantio: "If virtue no delighted beauty lack, / Your son-in-law is far more fair than black" (1.3.290-1). What might the Duke mean here by "fair"? What might he mean by "black"? Give at least two possibilities. Do you think the Duke is intending the words to have more than one meaning?

29. What parting advice does Brabantio give to Othello (1.3.293-4)? Quote and memorize the couplet that begins:

    "Look to her,_____

    _____."

30. How does Othello respond to Brabantio (1.3.295)? Quote his sentence that begins:

    "My life_____."

31. Othello calls his ancient, "Honest Iago" (1.3.295). In the 1600s *honest* could mean: "truthful, trustworthy" (*OED* 4a), "free from guile, straightforward, frank" (*OED* 4d); and "virtuous" (*OED* 3a). But *honest* also could be used "as a general epithet of appreciation or praise, esp. as used in a patronizing way to an inferior" (*OED* 2b).

    a. What do you think Othello intends the word to mean?

    b. How might Iago hear the term? If you were Iago, how would you feel about being called "Honest Iago"?

c. Can you think of a term in twenty-first century English that, like *honest* in the 1600s, can be used to praise but also to patronize or belittle?

32. What is making Roderigo feel like drowning himself (1.3.306)?

33. "I have looked upon the world for four times seven years" (1.3.312-13). How old is Iago? Do you think Roderigo is younger or older? Give a reason.

34. How does Iago respond to Roderigo's wanting to drown himself?

35. Iago explains, "Our bodies are gardens, to the which our wills are gardeners" (1.3.320-1). Analyze this metaphor:

       vehicle   :   tenor

       _____ :   bodies

       _____ :   will

Make a quick sketch of the extended description (1.3.321-5):

36. What does Iago assert about the effects of reason (1.3.325-31)?

37. Reread 1.3.333-75 ("It is merely a lust of the blood [. . .] I'll go sell all my land") and then answer the following:

    a. Iago tells Roderigo, "Put money in thy purse, follow thou the wars" (1.3.337-8). What do we eventually learn about how Roderigo will get or "make" the money to put in his purse? What does Roderigo say he will sell (1.3.375)?

    b. What is the effect of Iago's repetition, with variation, of his advice about Roderigo making money?

    c. What reason does Iago give that if Roderigo follows to Cyprus, he shall "enjoy" Desdemona (1.3.355)?

    d. How does Iago characterize Othello when he calls him "an erring barbarian" (1.3.352-3)? (*Barbarian* can mean "a native of Barbary [in North Africa]" (*OED* 5a), "a foreigner," (*OED* 1), and "a rude, wild, uncivilized person" (*OED* 3a); *erring* can mean "wandering" and also "deviating from the right [. . .] course" (*OED* a).)

    e. How does Iago characterize Desdemona when he calls her "a supersubtle Venetian" (1.3.353)? (*Subtle* can mean "discerning, shrewd" (*OED* 1) and "crafty, cunning, sly" (*OED* 2a).)

f. Once Roderigo leaves, what does Iago declare about why he would spend time "with such a snipe" (1.3.378)?

g. What new reason does Iago give for "hat[ing] the Moor" (1.3.379-83)?

h. How does Iago plan to "get [Cassio's] place" (1.3.386)? How will he "abuse Othello's ear" (1.3.389)?

i. What does Iago say now about Othello's nature (1.3.393-4)? Do you agree with Iago's assessment?

j. Consider the final couplet: "I have't. It is engendered. Hell and night / Must bring this monstrous birth to the world's light" (1.3.197-8). Earlier Iago has said to Roderigo, "There are many events in the womb of time which will be delivered" (1.3.366-7). What do these metaphors of pregnancy and birth imply about how Iago imagines his plan?

ACT 2, SCENE 1

1. As you read the opening conversation of Montano and the two Gentlemen (2.1.1-42), you will hear them describe what they are seeing as they look from the "cape" to the sea (2.1.1). Jot down two or three images that you find particularly striking:

2. EXTRA OPPORTUNITY. How would you stage the opening of this scene? Jot down some notes or draw and label a stage diagram.

3. According to Gentleman 3, how is it that "Our wars are done" (2.1.20)?

4. When Cassio arrives, why does he "loo[k] sadly" despite the Turkish loss (2.1.31-4)?

5. How does Montano know Othello? What does he say about him (2.1.34-6)?

6. What mood is created by the image of the empty town with all of its people standing "On the brow o' the sea" (2.1.53-4)?

7. How does Cassio describe Desdemona (2.1.61-5)?

8. What does Cassio imagine was the "divine" Desdemona's effect on the tempest (2.1.67-73)?

9. What might Cassio mean when he calls Desdemona "our great captain's captain" (2.1.74)?

10. What does Cassio mean when he says, "The riches of the ship is come on shore" (2.1.83)? What earlier comment (spoken by Iago) does this remark echo?

11. What do Cassio's various comments about Desdemona suggest about him?

12. When Cassio greets Emilia and attributes his "show of courtesy" (probably a kiss) toward another man's wife to his "breeding," Iago responds, "Sir, would she give you so much of her lips / As of her tongue she oft bestows on me, / You'd have enough" (2.1.100-3). Explain Iago's comment. With what tone might Iago say make this remark? What does it reveal about Iago? About his relationship to Emilia?

13. When Desdemona protests that Emilia "has no speech" (2.1.102), Iago says that she nonetheless "chides." How, according to Iago, does she do so (2.1.106-7)? (*Chide* means "To scold by way of rebuke" (*OED* 1c).)

14. Explain what Iago asserts about wives: "You are pictures out of doors [. . .] and housewives in your beds" (2.1.108-11)?

15. Iago answers Desdemona's accusation that he is a "slanderer" by saying, "Nay, it is true, or else I am a Turk" (2.1.113). What does Iago mean by "Turk"? What does he imply about Turks? (A *slanderer* is "one who [. . .] utters false or malicious statement about a person" (*OED* 1).)

16. If you were directing this scene, with what tone would you direct Iago to deliver his lines during this conversation with Desdemona and Emilia? Is he joking? Serious? How would you direct Desdemona and Emilia to respond to Iago?

17. EXTRA OPPORTUNITY. When Emilia tells Iago, "You shall not write my praise," Desdemona asks, "What wouldst thou write of me, if thou shouldst praise me?" (2.1.115-17). Imagine you are performing Desdemona: what could motivate Desdemona to ask this question?

18. Desdemona soon announces, "I am not merry, but I do beguile / The thing I am, by seeming otherwise" (2.1.121-2).

   a. First, explain what Desdemona is saying.

   b. What line of Iago's does it echo?

   c. Then consider staging: although there is no stage direction in either of the earliest texts, some editors of recent editions mark this line as "aside." How would you stage this moment? To whom does Desdemona speak? Explain your choice. *(See appendix 3, "On How an Edition of Othello Is Made," for an introduction to the early texts of Othello.)*

19. About what is Desdemona and Iago's exchange (2.1.123-59)? How do they use the words "fair" and "black"? What is the tone of their exchange? Notice the puns, such as wit/white/wight (2.1.131-2) (A *pun* is the use of a word in a statement that simultaneously suggests two or more meanings of the word and, thus, two or more ways to understand the statement.)

20. How does Iago describe "a deserving woman" (2.1.145-57)?

21. What final comment does Desdemona make (2.1.158)? What does she say to Emilia and Cassio?

22. What does Cassio mean when he says of Iago: "You may relish him more in the soldier than the scholar" (2.1.162-3)? If you were Iago, how would you feel hearing this comment? (Recall Iago's complaint about Othello's choice of Cassio for lieutenant.)

23. What does this conversation show about the relative social status of the speakers—Iago, Emilia, Desdemona, and Cassio?

24. "With as little a web as this, will I ensnare as great a fly as Cassio" (2.1.165-6):

    a. To what does *this* refer? (Review Iago's narration of how Cassio is treating Desdemona.)

    b. Analyze the metaphor by charting its vehicle and tenor:

       vehicle   :   tenor

    c. EXTRA OPPORTUNITY. Make a sketch that shows the metaphor's vehicle and tenor.

25. Why does Othello feel, "If it were now to die, / 'Twere now to be most happy" (2.1.184-5)?

26. How does Desdemona respond (2.1.188-9)?

27. What is the "music" to which Iago refers when he says that he will "set down the pegs that make this music" (2.1.195)? (*Peg* here likely refers to a tuning peg on a stringed instrument.)

28. How is the conflict with the Turks resolved?

29. Reread 2.1.215-40 ("Lay thy finger thus [. . .] the woman hath found him already"):

    a. How does Iago attempt to convince Roderigo that Desdemona "is directly in love" with Cassio (2.1.213)?

    b. Why, according to Iago, will Desdemona soon tire of Othello?

    c. What does Iago assert about Desdemona?

d. What does he assert about Othello?

e. According to Iago, why will Cassio be Desdemona's "second choice" (2.1.228)?

30. How does Roderigo respond to Othello's predictions about Desdemona?

31. EXTRA OPPORTUNITY. What twenty-first-century English expression could you substitute for "The wine she drinks is made of grapes" (2.1.243-4)?

32. When Roderigo interprets Desdemona's touching Cassio's hand as "courtesy," Iago counters, "Lechery, by this hand" (2.1.247-48). (*Lechery* means "habitual indulgence of lust" (*OED* 1); *courtesy* means "courtly elegance and politeness of manner" (*OED* 1).) What does Iago imply about how to understand intention from an observed action?

33. What does Iago instruct Roderigo to do? What's the plan? What do you think makes Roderigo agree to his part in it?

34. Reread Iago's soliloquy that ends the scene (2.1.275-301) and answer the following questions:

   a. What does Iago say about Othello's nature? About what kind of husband he'll be?

   b. How does Iago explain, "I do love her too" (2.1.280)? What motivates his "love" for Desdemona?

   c. What does Iago mean when he says he suspects, "the lusty Moor / Hath leaped into my seat" (2.1.284-5)?

   d. What does the thought of Othello having done so do to Iago? Quote the simile:

   e. How does Iago plan to get even?

   f. What will Iago achieve if "this poor trash of Venice" (Roderigo) "stand the putting on" (2.1.292)? What does Iago mean that he'll have Cassio "on the hip" (2.1.294)?

g. Of what does Iago accuse Cassio when he says, "For I fear Cassio with my night-cap too" (2.1.296)?

h. Explain: "Knavery's plain face is never seen till used" (2.1.301). (*Knavery* means "dishonest or crafty behaviour" (*OED* 1).)

i. By the speech's end, what new have you learned about Iago?

j. If you were performing Iago, would you speak this soliloquy as if to yourself or would you speak it directly to the play's audience? How would your choice affect the portrayal of Iago? How would it affect the audience's understanding of Iago's various claims?

ACT 2, SCENE 2

1. What does the herald proclaim? What happened to the Turkish fleet? What will be celebrated? Summarize his proclamation.

2. EXTRA OPPORTUNITY. If you were making a film version of *Othello* what music would you choose for this scene? What images would you show? Briefly explain your choices.

ACT 2, SCENE 3

1. Review the herald's proclamation about celebrations and then explain Othello's order to Cassio about the night's guard: "Let's teach ourselves that honorable stop, / Not to outsport discretion" (2.3.1-3). (*Discretion* means "demonstration of sound judgment" (*OED* 4a).)

2. Considering what you've heard from Iago, how do Cassio and Othello's comments about Iago make you feel?

3. Othello tells Desdemona, "Come, my dear love. / The purchase made, the fruits are to ensue: / That profit's yet to come 'tween me and you (2.3.8-10).

   a. With what kind of (figurative) language does Othello refer to their marriage and their night's activities? Underline key words or phrases in the passage quoted above, and then explain what they imply.

   b. EXTRA OPPORTUNITY. Some scholars read Othello's invitation as an indication that their marriage has not yet been consummated: they were awakened on the night they eloped in Venice and left immediately for Cyprus. (*Consummate* means "To make (a marriage) complete by the act of sexual intercourse" (*OED* 1).) Do you agree? What else could Othello mean?

4. How does Cassio respond to Iago's slanderous remarks about Desdemona?

5. Review 2.3.29-40. When Iago invites Cassio to share a stoup of wine, how does Cassio respond? What does Cassio say about drinking? What does Cassio say as he nonetheless agrees to invite the gallants to drink?

6. What does Iago say will be the effects of drinking on Cassio? Why is he so eager to have Cassio drink?

7. What does Iago say that love has done to Roderigo? Quote the phrase:

   "Whom love _____" (2.3.45).

8. EXTRA OPPORTUNITY. Analyze Iago's metaphor by charting its vehicle and tenor: "If consequence do but approve my dream, / My boat sails freely, both with wind and stream" (2.3.56-7).

   vehicle   :   tenor

   How does this metaphor compare to Iago's act 1, scene 1 metaphor that he "must be be-lee'd and calmed" (1.1.28)?

9. EXTRA OPPORTUNITY. How might the first audiences of *Othello* have responded to Iago's remarks about Englishmen drinking?

10. Is Cassio drunk? Quote what Cassio says that is the best clue and explain what you think it shows about his state.

11. In his conversation with Montano, how does Iago slander Cassio?

12. Is Iago's slander effective? Quote a key phrase (of Montano's response) from which you derive your answer.

13. Briefly explain what eventually happens that brings Othello back outside.

14. Consider Othello's question: "Are we turned Turks, and to ourselves do that / Which heaven hath forbid the Ottomites? / For Christian shame, put by this barbarous brawl" (2.3.154-6). To what does Othello attribute their having escaped the Ottomites' or Turks' attack? Of what does Othello imagine Christians being ashamed? What seems to be Othello's religion? Where have you heard other references to Turks or barbarians?

15. With what does Othello threaten "He that stirs next" (2.3.157)?

16. Analyze the metaphor Othello uses to describe what Montano has done to his reputation: "What's the matter / That you unlace your reputation thus, / And spend your rich opinion for the name / Of a night-brawler?" (2.3.177-80). (Note that in the 1600s, one would *unlace* the strings of one's purse; here *opinion* is a synonym for reputation (*OED* 3).)

    vehicle : tenor

    unlace : _____

    _____ : reputation (opinion)

    spend : _____

    rich : _____

    _____ : name of night-brawler

17. How does Iago respond to Othello's demand for information? What does he accomplish with this response? What does Othello assume about the report Iago gives (2.3.230-3)?

18. Explain what makes Cassio say that he is hurt "past all surgery" (2.3.244)? Do you agree that he is?

19. What does Iago say about reputation? Quote the key sentences and phrases. Do you agree with any part of what Iago says about reputation? Explain your reason.

20. EXTRA OPPORTUNITY. To what does Cassio refer when he says, "Oh God, that men should put an enemy in their mouths to steal away their brains" (2.3.270-1)? What is the "enemy"? Sketch Cassio's metaphor.

21. What does Iago mean when he says, "Our general's wife is now the general" (2.3.294-5)?

22. What advice does Iago give to Cassio about how to ask Othello to be reinstated?

23. What does Iago explain about his plan after Cassio leaves (2.3.311-39)? Answer the following from Iago's point of view:

   a. What about Desdemona makes his advice "free" and "honest" (2.3.312)? What will Desdemona naturally be inclined to do?

   b. Notice "were't to renounce his baptism" (2.3.319). What does this comment indicate about Othello's religion? (*Baptism* is an initiation ceremony into a Christian church.)

   c. Iago claims that Othello's "soul is so enfettered to her love / That she may make, unmake, do what she list" (2.3.321-2). (*Enfettered* means enchained or shackled; *list* here means pleases.) Make a quick sketch of this image.

   d. What about Othello will allow Desdemona's "appetite" to "play the god" (2.3.323)? Quote the phrase.

e. "When devils will the blackest sins put on / They do suggest at first with heavenly shows, / As I do now" (2.3.327-9). What does "blackest" mean here? Who, does Iago imply, is like a devil?

f. What "pestilence" will Iago pour into Othello's ear (2.3.332)? What would be the effect of pouring "pestilence" into someone's ear?

g. "And out of her own goodness make the net / That shall enmesh them all" (2.3.338-9). In Iago's plan, how will Desdemona's goodness become the net?

24. How does Iago convince Roderigo not to return to Venice? Explain: "Thou know'st we work by wit, and not by witchcraft, / And wit depends on dilatory time" (2.3.348-9). (*Dilatory* means "tending to cause delay" (*OED* 1a).)

25. How will Iago involve his wife, Emilia, in his plan?

ACT 3, SCENE 1

Find a partner and read aloud the conversations between the Clown and the Musician and the Clown and Cassio. Listen for how the Clown's jokes work.

1. What is the nature of the Clown's jokes? How, for example, does the Clown imply the music sounds when he asks, "Are these, I pray you, wind instruments?" (3.1.6)? If you were playing the Clown, what word would you emphasize to get the joke across to an audience?

2. Consider Cassio's asking the Clown to ""keep up [his] quillets" (3.1.23). (*Keep up* here likely means "to keep shut up" or "to keep secret" (*OED* 1, 2); a *quillet* is a quibble or play-on-words.)

    Cassio Dost thou hear, mine honest friend?
    Clown No, I hear not your honest friend. I hear you.
    Cassio Pr'ythee, keep up thy quillets. (3.1.21-3)

   Explain the Clown's quillet (play-on-words) to which Cassio refers.

3. What is the effect of a scene with clowning of this sort following act 2, scene 3?

4. Who is "the gentlewoman that attends the General's wife" (3.1.24-5)? Why has Cassio sent for her?

5. After Iago departs, Cassio remarks, "I never knew / A Florentine more kind and honest" (3.1.39-40). What meaning(s) of *honest* do you think Cassio intends here? Give your reasons. *(For a list of seventeenth-century definitions of* honest, *see Larger Question 1, "Honesty," on page 1.)*

6. What does Emilia tell Cassio is the reason that Othello "might not but refuse you" (3.1.47)? What does Emilia say is the only "suitor" Othello needs to "bring [Cassio] in again" (3.1.49)?

ACT 3, SCENE 2

1. What news might Othello be sending to the Senate in the letters that he gives to Iago?

2. If you were making a film of *Othello*, how would you shoot this scene? What might you want to provoke your audience to think about as Othello is "walking on the works" (3.2.3) and checking the fortification of the island as he entrusts his business to Iago? (*Works* can mean "a defensive structure, a fortification (*OED* 14).) Make a sketch and jot down some ideas.

ACT 3, SCENE 3

1. The scene begins in the middle of Cassio's conversation with Desdemona. What might Cassio have said right before the scene begins? Imagining how he speaks and what he might have said, write a line for him:

2. Explain the dramatic irony in Emilia's line: "I warrant it grieves my husband / As if the cause were his" (3.3.3-4). (*Dramatic irony* occurs when the audience or a character has more information than another character.)

3. What does Desdemona mean when she tells Cassio that Othello "shall in strangeness stand no further off / Than in a politic distance" (3.3.12-13)?

4. Desdemona tells Cassio, "Before Emilia here / I give thee warrant of thy place" (3.3.19-20)? (*Warrant* here means "assurance given, pledge" (*OED* 4b).)

   a. Of what must Desdemona be confident to assure Cassio of his place as lieutenant?

   b. If you were Othello, how would you feel if you knew Desdemona had done so?

5. Analyze Desdemona's metaphor that describes how she will go about persuading Othello: "My lord shall never rest, / I'll watch him tame" (3.1.22-3). (*Watch* here means "to keep awake intentionally (*OED* 1b). Keeping awake a captured wild animal, such as a falcon, is a technique for taming it.)

vehicle	:	tenor
_____	:	Othello
_____	:	Desdemona
tame	:	_____

6. Imagine you are performing Desdemona. What is your motivation here? For what reasons might you be so intent on compelling Othello to reinstate Cassio as lieutenant? Give at least two possibilities.

7. Why does Cassio depart even when Desdemona encourages him to stay?

8. Notice how Iago begins to portray Cassio as having improper contact with Desdemona. Consider for instance, "I cannot think it / That he would steal away so guilty-like, / Seeing you coming" (3.3.39-41). Is Iago's observation of Cassio's action accurate? (Does Cassio steal away guiltily?) Explain Iago's strategy.

9. When Othello agrees to call Cassio but doesn't agree to a specific time, Desdemona eventually asks, "I wonder in my soul / What you would ask me, that I should deny" (3.3.69-70). What does she then emphasize about what Cassio did for Othello (3.3.71-4)?

10. "Prythee, no more. Let him come when he will. / I will deny thee nothing" (3.3.76-7)? What does Othello's eventual response indicate is his reason for agreeing to see Cassio?

11. How, according to Desdemona, is her effort to have him reinstate Cassio "not a boon" (3.3.77)? (*Boon* here means "a favour, a gift" (*OED* 4).)

12. Explain Othello's statement about Desdemona: "Perdition catch my soul, / But I do love thee! And when I love thee not, / Chaos is come again" (3.3.91-3). What does Othello reveal about how he experiences the effect on his life of his love for Desdemona? (*Perdition* means "utter destruction" (*OED* 1).)

13. How does Iago continue to execute his plan? Think about how you would deliver your lines if you were performing Iago. For example, with what tone might you ask "Indeed?" when Othello says that when he was courting Desdemona, Cassio "went between [them] very oft" (3.3.101-2)? Try performing the question in a few ways.

14. To what does Othello compare Iago's echoing responses? Quote the phrase: "As if there were

    _____" (3.3.108-9).

15. How does Othello describe the way Iago pursed his brow (3.3.114)? Quote the phrase: "As if thou

    then _____" (3.3.115-16).

16. Consider Othello's remarks that you have quoted above. Is Othello accurately observing Iago? Is Othello understanding accurately what he observes? Explain your answer.

17. Reread what Othello says to Iago:

    > And for I know thou'rt full of love and honesty
    > And weigh'st thy words before thou giv'st them breath,
    > Therefore these stops of thine fright me the more.
    > For such things in a false disloyal knave
    > Are tricks of custom. But in a man that's just,
    > They're close dilations, working from the heart,
    > That passion cannot rule. (3.3.119-125)

    a. Explain what Othello says about what "these stops" (the pauses in Iago's speech) mean in a "false disloyal knave" and what they mean in a "man that's just"?

    b. What, then, keeps Othello from concluding from his observations of Iago's speech and behavior that Iago is planning something horrible?

18. When Othello orders Iago to "give [his] worst of thoughts / The worst of words," Iago begs his pardon and explains, "Though I am bound to every act of duty, / I am not bound to that all slaves are free to. / Utter my thoughts?" (3.3.133-7). What does Iago emphasize about speech? What does he say even slaves are free to do?

19. What likely motivates Iago to "confess" that it is his "nature's plague / To spy into abuses, and of [his] jealousy / Shape faults that are not" (3.3.147-9)?

20. What does Iago say is "the immediate jewel" of men and women's "souls" (3.3.157)? What is Iago's strategy in saying this?

21. With what metaphor does Iago describe jealousy (3.3.167-8)? Quote the sentence.

22. Explain what Iago says about two different kinds of cuckolds (3.3.168-71). (A *cuckold* is "a derisive name for the husband of an unfaithful wife" (*OED* 1).) What does Iago emphasize about doubt and suspicion?

23. What does Othello mean when he says, "Nor from mine own weak merits will I draw / The smallest fear or doubt of her revolt, / For she had eyes, and chose me" (3.3.188-90)?

24. List the sequence of actions Othello says he would take if he suspected his wife of infidelity (3.3.190-3). Note that *doubt* can mean "suspect."

25. What advice does Iago give Othello?

26. "I know our country disposition well. / In Venice they do let heaven see the pranks / They dare not show their husbands. Their best conscience / Is not to leave undone, but keep unknown" (3.3.202-5). What does Iago say here about Venetian women? Why might this assertion be persuasive to Othello?

27. When Iago says, "She did deceive her father, marrying you" (3.3.207), what might Othello remember that Brabantio had said to him?

28. With what evidence does Iago argue that Desdemona is capable of deception (3.3.208-9)?

29. Consider Iago's metaphor below. (*Seel* means "to make blind" (*OED* 2). While taming hawks, falconers seeled their hawks' eyes by sewing the lids together. Although spelled *seal* in some modern editions (including the Yale edition quoted below), both earliest editions print *seel*.)

    She that, so young, could give such a seeming,
    To seal her father's eyes up close as oak,
    He thought 'twas witchcraft. (3.3.211-13)

vehicle	:	tenor
_____	:	She (Desdemona)
_____	:	father's (Brabantio's)
seel eyes	:	_____

    What does the metaphor imply?

    What metaphor that Desdemona spoke to Cassio does Iago's metaphor recall?

30. What does Othello likely mean when he tells Iago, "I am bound to thee forever" (3.3.215)? In what way is he bound to Iago that he does not yet understand?

31. Reread Iago's speech at 3.3.230-9 ("Not to affect many proposed matches [. . .] And happily repent"). What does Iago suggest about a woman who would not "affect" a "match" (a husband) "Of her own clime, complexion, and degree" (3.3.230-1)? (Here *affect* means "seek" or "show preference for"(*OED* 1, 4a).) What does Iago say may happen to her "will" when she "recoil[s] to her better judgment" (3.3.237)?

32. How, then, does Iago attempt to make Othello doubt Desdemona's love and faithfulness?

33. When Iago reenters, what does he advise Othello to do about Cassio (3.3.245-56)? What's Iago's strategy here?

34. Analyze the metaphor below. (When properly tamed, a hawk will bring captured prey back to its falconer. A *haggard* hawk is not sufficiently tame and, thus, might eat the prey it hunts rather than return it to the falconer. *Jesses* are leather leashes used while a falconer is training a hawk.)

> If I do prove her haggard,
> Though that her jesses were my dear heartstrings,
> I'd whistle her off and let her down the wind
> To prey at fortune (3.3.260-3)

vehicle	:	tenor
_____	:	I (Othello)
_____	:	her (Desdemona)
haggard	:	_____
jesses	:	_____
let her down the wind	:	_____
to prey	:	_____
_____	:	fortune

35. What three possible reasons does Othello imagine for his wife's unfaithfulness? List them.

36. Explain what Othello means when he says that the "curse of marriage" is "That we can call these delicate creatures ours, / And not their appetites" (3.3.268-70). Who is "we"? What "appetite" does he imagine he cannot call "ours"?

37. What does Othello say about destiny and "this forkèd plague" of being a cuckold (3.3.273-7)?

38. What does Othello say when he sees Desdemona (3.3.278-9)?

39. What is Desdemona doing with her "napkin" (her handkerchief) when she loses it?

40. Why is Emilia glad to find the napkin?

41. What does she say is the reason Desdemona loves it and always keep it with her?

42. If Emilia knows Desdemona loves this handkerchief, why might she nonetheless grant Iago's request to steal it and give it to him? Give two or three possibilities.

43. What more do we learn about Emilia and Iago's relationship from their exchange about the handkerchief (3.3.300-19)?

44. EXTRA OPPORTUNITY. In printing Iago and Emilia's exchange at 3.3.313-18, the editor of the 2005 Yale edition adds stage directions not in either of the early texts of *Othello*—"*not giving it*" and "*snatches it*").

> Iago A good wench, give it me.
> Emilia (*not giving it*) What will you do with't, that you have been so earnest
>   To have me filch it?
> Iago   (*snatches it*) Why, what is that to you?
> Emilia If it be not for some purpose of import,
>   Give't me again. Poor lady, she'll run mad
>   When she shall lack it.

Think of an alternative way actors might perform these lines. How else and when might Iago get the handkerchief? Insert directions below in the empty parentheses.

> Iago (   )A good wench, give it me.
>
> Emilia (   )What will you do with't, that you have been so earnest
>   To have me filch it?
>
> Iago (   )Why, what is that to you?
>
> Emilia (   ) If it be not for some purpose of import,
>
>   Give't me again. Poor lady, she'll run mad
>
>   When she shall lack it.

Explain what the difference in staging would suggest about Emilia's and Iago's characters.

45. What does Iago plan to do with the handkerchief?

46. Memorize these lines: "Trifles light as air / Are to the jealous confirmations strong / As proofs of holy writ" (3.3.321-3). Do you agree? Why or why not?

47. How, according to Iago, are "dangerous conceits" (or thoughts) like poisons (3.3.325-8)?

48. What does Iago's description of Othello ("Look where he comes. Not poppy, nor mandragora, / Nor all the drowsy syrups of the world, / Shall ever medicine thee to that sweet sleep / Which thou ow'dst yesterday" (3.3.330-3) indicate about how Othello acts as he enters?

49. Do you agree with Othello's statement about robbery: "He that is robbed, not wanting what is stolen / Let him not know't, and he's not robbed at all" (3.3.342-3)? Why or why not?

50. To what does Othello bid farewell?

51. What does Othello mean when he commands: "Give me the ocular proof" (3.3.360)? How does Othello threaten Iago?

52. What is Iago's purpose in saying: "O wretchèd fool, / That liv'st to make thine honesty a vice" (3.3.375-6)? Who is the fool to whom he refers?

53. Explain Othello's assertion: "My name, that was as fresh / As Dian's visage, is now begrimed and black / As mine own face" (3.3.386-8). (*Dian* is a name for the moon; *visage* means "face.") Which color terms are literal? Which figurative?

54. What does Iago assume when he asks Othello, "Would you [. . .] grossly gape on? / Behold her topped" (3.3.395-6)? How does Iago circumvent Othello's demand for "ocular proof"?

55. What story does Iago tell to give Othello "a living reason" that Desdemona has been unfaithful (3.3.413-25)? What do you think about this story? What does it show about Iago? How does Othello respond? What does this response show about Othello?

56. What is Iago's approach to Othello's demand for "proof"? Explain: "And this may help to thicken other proofs / That do demonstrate thinly" (3.3.429-30).

57. Othello compares his bloody thoughts to the Pontic Sea (3.3.453-60). What does this simile, with its extended description of the Pontic Sea, reveal about how Othello feels about his bloody thoughts of revenge?

58. What does Othello vow? What does Iago vow in response? What are they doing physically as they speak these vows?

59. What does Othello order Iago to do? What position does he give Iago?

60. Review the scene. What makes it possible for Iago to persuade Othello that Desdemona and Cassio have betrayed him? Jot down some ideas about what each character could have done—or not done—to help avoid this outcome:

    Othello

    Desdemona

    Cassio

    Emilia

ACT 3, SCENE 4

1. Why would Desdemona call Cassio "Lieutenant Cassio" even though he is no longer lieutenant (3.4.1)? Give two or three possibilities.

2. Reread 3.4.1-13. How does the Clown pun on the verb *to lie*?

3. What is the effect of this kind of clowning at this point in the play?

4. Why, according to Desdemona, would she rather have lost her "purse / Full of crusadoes" than have lost her handkerchief (3.4.23-4)?

5. How does Desdemona answer Emilia's question, "Is he not jealous" (3.4.27)?

6. What story does Othello tell Desdemona about the handkerchief's origin (3.4.53-73)? Summarize it.

7. What stories that we heard earlier in the play does this story remind you of?

8. With what tone might Desdemona speak the line, "Is't possible" (3.4.66) and then the line, "Indeed? Is't true" (3.4.74)? Recite each in two different ways.

9. Imagine you are performing Desdemona: what is your motivation to lie and say the handkerchief is not lost? Give two possibilities.

10. What do Desdemona's attempts to change the subject to Cassio add to this scene?

11. Imagine you are performing Emilia: what is your motivation not to tell Desdemona that you found the handkerchief? Give two possibilities.

12. Analyze Emilia's metaphor by sorting its vehicle and tenor.

    'Tis not a year or two shows us a man.
    They are all but stomachs and we all but food,
    They eat us hungerly, and when they are full
    They belch us. (3.4.101-4)

    vehicle   :   tenor

13. As Cassio and Iago enter, what advice is Iago giving Cassio (3.4.105-6)? (*Importune* means "to ask or request something of (a person) persistently or pressingly [. . .] to beg, beseech" (*OED* 1).)

14. How does Desdemona explain why Cassio "must awhile be patient" (3.4.127)? What does she mean when she says, "My advocation is not now in tune" (3.4.121)? Where have you heard the imagery of tuning before?

15. What is the effect of Iago's repeatedly asking if Othello is angry and of describing violent anger in the metaphor about "the cannon" (3.4.130-7)?

16. What does Desdemona conclude must have "puddled" Othello's "clear spirit" (3.4.141)?

17. To what does Desdemona compare the effects of an aching finger: "For let our finger ache, and it indues / Our other healthful members even to that sense / Of pain" (3.4.144-6)? What does she imagine is Othello's aching finger? What the other healthful parts of his body?

18. When Desdemona says, "I never gave him cause" to be jealous (3.4.156), what does Emilia explain about the nature of jealousy? With what metaphor does Emilia describe jealousy? Quote it.

19. How does Cassio greet Bianca? How does he speak to her (3.4.168-70)?

20. About what does Bianca complain?

21. What does Cassio ask Bianca to do with the handkerchief? What does Bianca suspect about it (3.4.180-1)?

22. How does Cassio explain to Bianca why he wants her to "leave [him] for this time" (3.4.190)? (Consider: "I do atttend here on the general, / And think it not addition, nor my wish, / To have him see me womaned" (3.4.192-4).) What does Cassio reveal is his attitude toward Bianca?

23. What does Bianca accomplish with her response to Cassio's "Not that I love you not": "But that you do not love me" (3.4.195-6)?

24. What do we learn about Cassio and Bianca's relationship?

ACT 4, SCENE 1

1. What are Othello and Iago talking about as the scene opens?

2. Consider and explain Iago's paradoxical remark about a wife's honor: "Her honor is an essence that's not seen: / They have it very oft that have it not" (4.1.16-17). If honor is "not seen,"—invisible—then how, according to Iago, can someone "have" honor who doesn't have it?

3. With what simile does Othello describe how the handkerchief "comes o'er [his] memory" (4.1.19-22)? Quote it.

4. What exactly does Iago tell Othello about Cassio?

5. What happens to the way Othello speaks just before he falls into a trance (4.1.34-42)?

6. What does Othello mean when he says, "It is not words that shake me thus" (4.1.40-1)? What does Othello imply shakes him? What do you think shakes Othello?

7. "Work on. / My medicine works" (4.1.43-4). What is Iago's "medicine"?

8. How does Iago describe Othello when speaking to Cassio (4.1.49-54)? Quote key words and phrases.

9. When Iago encourages Othello to "bear [his] fortune like a man," Othello responds, "a hornèd man's a monster and a beast" (4.1.60-1)? (*Cuckolds* were described as having horns.) What does Othello say about what having an unfaithful wife turns him into? How had Iago described Othello (in the very first scene of the play) when alarming Brabantio about his daughter's marriage?

10. What, according to Iago, is "better" about Othello's "case" of suspecting his wife of being unfaithful (4.1.68)?

11. What does Iago imply when he says, "let me know, / And knowing what I am, I know what she shall be" (4.1.71-2)? What does Iago imply his wife would "be" if he knew that she was unfaithful?

12. What does Iago tell Othello he will discuss with Cassio while Othello observes and "mark[s] his gesture" (4.1.87)? What, in fact, will Iago question Cassio about?

13. Note that Iago says that Bianca sells "her desires" in order to "buy herself bread and clothes" and that she "dotes on Cassio" (4.1.94-6). What does Iago mean when he says that it's "the strumpet's plague / To beguile many and be beguiled by one" (4.1.96-7)? (A *strumpet* is a prostitute; to *beguile* is to deceive.) Whom, according to Iago, does Bianca beguile? By whom is she beguiled?

14. How would you stage this part of act 4, scene 1, where Cassio and Iago speak about Bianca and Othello watches and comments? Make a sketch or diagram of who would be where on the stage and where the play's audience would be.

15. What does Othello conclude from what he sees? What leads him to draw this incorrect conclusion?

16. During his conversation with Iago (4.1.103-42), what attitude does Cassio express toward Bianca? Start by quoting one or two key phrases from which you then derive your answer.

17. When Bianca enters, of what does she accuse Cassio? What has she concluded about the handkerchief she returns to Cassio?

18. With what tone might Cassio say, "How now, my sweet Bianca? How now? how now?" (4.1.151)? Try performing these lines in two different ways.

19. About what is Cassio concerned that makes him decide he "must" follow after Bianca (4.1.156)?

20. How does Othello speak about Desdemona now? What talents does Othello describe that prompt Iago to remark, "She's the worse for all this" (4.1.183)?

21. Why specifically does Othello ask Iago for poison (4.1.196)? What does Iago suggest instead? How might "the justice of it" please Othello (4.1.201)?

22. What does Iago mean when he says, "And for Cassio, let me be his undertaker" (4.1.202)?

23. What news does Lodovico bring in the letters from Venice (4.1.226)? How might this news make Othello feel at this point?

24. How does Othello treat Desdemona in front of Lodovico? What is Lodovico's reaction? What is Desdemona's reaction?

25. To what does Othello refer when he says, "O well-painted passion" (4.1.249)? Whose "passion"? What does he mean that the passion is "well-painted"?

26. What does Lodovico emphasize about Othello's behavior (4.1.257-61)? What does Lodovico suspect has happened to Othello? Quote key phrases from which you derive your answer.

27. What does Iago accomplish in his conversation with Lodovico after Othello exits?

28. What is the effect of Lodovico's appearance at this point in the play?

ACT 4, SCENE 2

1. Emilia wishes "the serpent's curse" on any "wretch" who might have made Othello suspicious of Desdemona (4.2.15-16). What does the serpent do that leads God to curse him? How does God curse the serpent? (If you are unfamiliar with this story, you can find it in Chapter 3 of the Bible's Book of Genesis.) How is Emilia's wish fitting?

2. After Emilia leaves, what comment does Othello make about Emilia's report on Desdemona (4.2.20-21)? What comment does he make about Desdemona (4.2.21-3)? Quote the key phrases.

3. As Desdemona struggles to understand why Othello thinks her false, she asks, "Why do you weep? / Am I the motive of these tears, my lord?" (4.2.42-3). Why might Othello weep? What other clues are there for how Othello is acting during the scene?

4. Desdemona wonders if Othello suspects her father is "an instrument" of Othello's "calling back" to Venice and assures her husband that she is not to blame, adding, "If you have lost him, / Why, I have lost him too" (4.2.44-7). What does Desdemona imagine could be a reason that Othello is unhappy with her?

5. Reread Othello's complicated speech at 4.2.47-64 ("Had it pleased heaven [. . .] grim as hell").

    a. What does Othello say he could have suffered and still have "found in some place of [his] soul / A drop of patience" (4.2.52-3)?

    b. EXTRA OPPORTUNITY. Try to visualize the metaphor Othello uses to describe feeling scorned: "But, alas, to make me / A fixèd figure for the time, for scorn / To point his slow and moving finger at!" (4.2.53-5). On what object associated with time is the slow and moving finger? Where would Othello be as a "fixèd figure"? Try sketching this image that associates scorn with "the time."

    c. What might Othello mean when he says, "But there where I have garnered up my heart" (4.2.57)? How is he distinguishing this place?

    d. What does Othello imagine "Patience, thou young and rose-lipp'ed cherubin" looking at (4.2.63)? What does he imagine is the effect? (A *cherubin* is an angel.)

    e. What do we learn from this speech about the nature of what Othello suffers? About what he cannot bear to suffer?

6. Analyze Othello's metaphor: "Was this fair paper, this most goodly book, / Made to write 'whore' upon" (4.2.71)? Chart its vehicle and tenor.

   vehicle   :   tenor

7. Notice: "I took you for that cunning whore of Venice / That married with Othello" (4.2.90-1). With what does Othello associate Venice now?

8. Note what Othello says to Emilia at the start and end of his meeting with Desdemona. When he asks Emilia to leave him and Desdemona, he says: "Some of your function, mistress. / Leave procreants alone and shut the door" (4.2.27-8). When Othello calls Emilia back, he says, "We have done our course. There's money for your pains. / I pray you turn the key, and keep our counsel" (4.2.94-5). How does Othello imagine his meeting with Desdemona arranged by her maid Emilia? (A *procreant* is one who procreates—begets or produces children (*OED* 1); *to keep counsel* means to keep secret (*OED* 5d).)

9. Why might Desdemona ask Emilia, "Lay on my bed my wedding sheets" (4.2.105)? Give two possibilities.

10. In what tone might Desdemona say, "'Tis meet I should be used so, very meet" (4.2.107)? Why might she think it is "meet"? (*Meet* here means "fitting"(*OED* 2b); *used* means "treated.")

11. What does Emilia emphasize about what Desdemona "forsook" only to be called a whore (4.2.125-7)?

12. What kind of person does Emilia insist has devised the slander that Desdemona has been unfaithful? What does Emilia imagine has motivated this person?

13. How does Iago respond to Emilia's expressed outrage (4.2.144, 148)?

14. For what advice does Desdemona ask Iago (4.2.148-9)?

15. "I cannot say whore. / It does abhor me now I speak the word" (4.2.161-2). What is the effect of Desdemona's pun on whore/abhor? What does she go on to say about doing the act that might earn her the "addition" of whore (4.2.163-4)? (*Abhor* means "to regard with disgust or hatred" (*OED* 2); *addition* means "title" (*OED* 4).)

16. How does Iago explain Othello's chiding Desdemona (4.2.165-7)?

17. What does Roderigo mean when he tells Iago, "I have heard too much. And your words and performances are no kin together" (4.2.182)?

18. What do we learn Roderigo has given Iago to give to Desdemona? What has Iago done with the gifts?

19. What does Roderigo announce that he is going to tell Desdemona?

20. How does Iago distract Roderigo from his plan? How do you account for Iago's success?

ACT 4, SCENE 3

1. What does Emilia's question, "Dismiss me?" suggest (4.3.13)? If you were performing Emilia, what would you be thinking as you asked this question?

2. How does Desdemona respond to Emilia's wish that Desdemona had never seen Othello (4.3.18)?

3. What does Desdemona ask Emilia to do if she dies before Emilia (4.3.23-4)?

4. What story does Desdemona tell about her mother's maid? What song will not "go from [Desdemona's] mind" (4.3.25-32)?

5. What is the effect, at this particular time, of Desdemona and Emilia's exchange about Lodovico (4.3.35-9)?

6. What question does Desdemona ask Emilia about women (4.3.61-3)?

7. How does Emilia respond to Desdemona's question, "Wouldst thou do such a deed for all the world" (4.3.65)? To what deed does Desdemona refer? What joke does Emilia make on "heavenly light" (4.3.68)?

8. Explain the logic of Emilia's rhetorical question, "Who would not make her husband a cuckold to make him a monarch?" (4.3.78-9). If you were performing Emilia, with what tone would you speak these lines?

9. How does Emilia back up her assertion, "But I do think it is their husbands' fault / If wives do fall" (4.3.89-9)? What does she mean by "The ills we do, their ills instruct us so" (4.3.105)?

10. For what does Desdemona pray in the couplet that ends the scene (4.3.106-7)?

ACT 5, SCENE 1

1. Roderigo says, "I have no great devotion to the deed, / And yet he hath given me satisfying reasons" (5.1.8-9). To what "deed" does Roderigo refer? What does Roderigo's comment reveal about the limits of reason?

2. Explain Iago's metaphor about Roderigo: "I have rubbed this young quat almost to the sense, / And he grows angry" (5.1.11-12). (A *quat* is a "pimple" or "small boil" (*OED* 1); *sense* can mean "liability to feel bodily pain or discomfort" (*OED* 18); *angry* can mean "inflamed [. . .] as a sore" (*OED* 8).)

3. What are the advantages for Iago if Roderigo and Cassio both are killed?

4. What happens when Roderigo attacks Cassio? Who stabs whom? How does Othello understand Cassio's cries?

5. Whom does Othello address when he says, "Minion, your dear lies dead, / And your unbless'd fate hies. Strumpet, I come" (5.1.33-4)?

6. Explain Othello's couplet: "Forth of my heart those charms, thine eyes, are blotted. / Thy bed, lust-stained, shall with lust's blood be spotted" (5.1.35-6). What does Othello imply about the effect of Desdemona's eyes? How does Othello think Desdemona's bed has been "lust-stained"? How will it be spotted with "lust's blood"?

7. Under what pretense does Iago kill Roderigo? Does Roderigo understand what has happened before he dies? Quote the phrase from which you derive your answer.

8. How does Bianca react to the wounded Cassio? How does Iago treat her? What does Iago mean when he says, "Gentlemen all, I do suspect this trash / To be a party in this injury—" (5.1.85-6)?

9. What is Iago insinuating when he twice asks, "Look you pale?" (5.1.104-5)? What do you think causes Bianca's paleness?

10. What does Iago say about "guiltiness" (5.1.109-110)? Quote it:

11. To what does "this" refer in Iago's assessment: "This is the fruits of whoring" (5.1.116)?

12. What does Emilia call Bianca? How does Bianca respond (5.2.121-3)?

ACT 5, SCENE 2

1. Read through Othello's speech that opens the scene (5.1.1-22). Then reread it, answering the questions below as you go:

    a. "It is the cause" (5.1.1). What is the cause?

    b. What does Othello's repeating "it is the cause" and insisting, "Let me not name it to you, you chaste stars" (5.1.2) indicate about how he is thinking and feeling about his intention to kill Desdemona?

    c. For what reason will Othello not shed Desdemona's blood (5.2.1-5)?

    d. Why, according to Othello, "must" Desdemona die (5.2.6)? What do you think of Othello's reason here?

    e. Explain what Othello says about putting out the light (of the candle or torch) versus putting out the light of Desdemona's life.

    f. What other metaphor does Othello speak to describe killing Desdemona (5.2.13-14)?

    g. What "almost persuade[s] / Justice to break her sword" (5.2.16-17)?

    h. "So sweet was ne'er so fatal" (5.2.20). What can *fatal* mean here? Give two possibilities.

2. Why does Othello ask Desdemona if she has "prayed tonight" (5.2.24)? What does Othello mean when he says, "I would not kill thy soul" (5.2.32)? What kind of prayer is he encouraging?

3. EXTRA OPPORTUNITY. Scan the iambic pentameter line that Othello starts and Desdemona finishes. *(For an explanation of "iambic pentameter" and instructions about scanning, see appendix 1, pages 87-89.)*

   Othello   Think on thy sins.

   Desdemona   They are loves I bear to you. (5.2.40)

   What variation(s) do you notice in the meter? What is the effect?

4. Consider Othello's logic: "thou dost stone my heart, / And mak'st me call what I intend to do / A murder, which I thought a sacrifice" (5.2.63-5).

   a. First, explain how Othello could think of killing Desdemona as a "sacrifice"? Sacrifice to what or for what? (*Sacrifice* can mean anything "offered to God or a deity as an act of propitiation or homage" (*OED* 2) or "The destruction or surrender of something valued or desired for the sake of something having, or regarded as having, a higher or a more pressing claim" (*OED* 4a).)

   b. What "stones'" Othello's heart?

   c. What does Othello imply about what would make him want to "murder" Desdemona?

   d. What does he imply about what would make him want to "sacrifice" her?

5. What event does Othello likely remember when he asserts that Cassio "hath confessed" (5.2.68)? Did Cassio confess to having done anything wrong with Desdemona?

6. With what image does Othello describe his "stomach" for revenge against Cassio (5.2.74-5)?

7. If you were performing Desdemona, what might you imagine to be your motivation for asking Othello, "Kill me tomorrow" (5.2.80)?

8. What clues are there (in Othello's lines) for how Desdemona reacts physically? Consider, for instance, "Down, strumpet!" and "Nay, if you strive" (5.2.79, 81). (*Strive* could mean "to fight" (*OED* 4).)

9. "I that am cruel am yet merciful" (5.2.86). How does Othello, as he kills his wife, imagine himself and his actions?

10. What does Othello imply should cause "a huge eclipse / Of sun and moon, and that the affrighted globe / Should yawn at alteration" (5.2.99-101)? What does this thought suggest about how Othello feels about what he has done?

11. What, according to Othello, is the result of "the very error of the moon" that "makes men mad" (5.2.109-10)? What might this remark imply he thinks or feels about what he has just done to Desdemona?

12. Note that Desdemona asserts, "A guiltless death I die" (5.2.122). Why might she then answer, "Nobody. I myself" to Emilia's asking, "who hath done this deed" (5.2.123-4)? Give two or three possible motivations.

13. How does Othello interpret the dying Desdemona's remark? Of what does he accuse Desdemona?

14. How does Emilia respond to Othello's report that her husband said Desdemona was false?

15. With what kind of language does Emilia refer to Othello and to Desdemona's marriage to him? Quote key phrases.

16. What is Emilia willing to risk in order to speak the truth?

17. How does Iago respond to Emilia's challenging him and speaking about the murder? Note that Gratiano exclaims, "Fie! Your sword upon a woman?" (5.2.223).

18. Why is Gratiano glad that Desdemona's father is dead? What, according to Gratiano, caused his death (5.2.203-8)?

19. What does Othello say now about the handkerchief (5.2.215-16)? What had he told Desdemona about the handkerchief earlier? Which story do you believe? What does the inconsistency suggest about Othello as a story-teller?

20. What prompts Iago to stab Emilia?

21. What might Othello mean when he asks, "But why should honor outlive honesty" (5.2.244)?

22. Othello asks, "O vain boast, / Who can control his fate?" (5.2.263-4), and he calls Desdemona "ill-starred wench" (5.2.271). Why might he speak of fate?

23. What does Othello invite as the consequence for what he has done (5.2.276-9)?

24. What, according to Othello, will make it impossible for him to kill Iago? Why does he want Iago to live (5.2.285-9)?

25. Othello asks to be spoken of as "An honorable murderer" and explains, "For naught did I in hate, but all in honor" (5.2.293-4). If you were performing Othello, what would you be thinking as you said this? How would you be feeling about honor? With what tone would you speak these lines?

26. Notice Iago's final lines in the play: "Demand me nothing. What you know, you know. / From this time forth, I never will speak word" (5.2.302-3). Consider the effect of Iago's refusal to speak. How does it affect the other characters? How does it affect us, the audience, and our understanding of his character and the play?

27. What letters does Lodovico find? What is the effect of these letters and papers serving as proof of what has happened?

28. To what position does Lodovico appoint Cassio?

29. What does Lodovico say will happen to Iago?

30. What might Othello be hoping for when he asks Lodovico: "Speak of me as I am" (5.2.341)? How does he go on to describe that he is? Derive your answer from key phrases.

31. EXTRA OPPORTUNITY. In the Yale edition of the play, Othello compares himself to "the base Judean" (5.2.346). The Yale edition follows the 1623 Folio, but some editions follow the 1622 Quarto where the line reads, "the base Indian." *(See appendix 3, "On How an Edition of Othello Is Made," for an explanation of how the differences in editions come about.)* If you were making an edition of *Othello*, which phrase would you pick? Explain what meanings you think it conveys and why you would choose it.

32. Analyze Othello's final metaphor (5.2.351-5). Who is the "malignant and a turbaned Turk"? Who is the Venetian? Who is the circumcisèd dog?

33. What is Othello's language like in his final speech? What does he accomplish before and as he kills himself?

34. "The object poisons sight, / Let it be hid" (5.2.363-4). To what object does Lodovico refer? What does Lodovico suggest about sight?

APPENDIX 1. LISTENING FOR METER—AN INTRODUCTION

Actors have long observed that Shakespeare's plays convey their meanings not only through the sense of his language but also through its sounds, including rhyme, consonance (repeated consonant sounds), assonance (repeated vowel sounds), and alliteration (repeated initial sounds). As you read the play, read speeches aloud and consider how the sounds contribute to their meanings.

This section will help you get started listening for the rhythms of a Shakespeare play by introducing you to meters you will encounter in *Othello*.

> ❧ For most English literature, **METER** refers to a deliberate pattern of stressed and unstressed syllables.
>
> *"Stressed" syllables are the syllables that get the most emphasis when a word or sentence is spoken aloud. (In the literature of some other languages, including Greek and Latin, meter is measured by the length rather than the stress of syllables.)*
>
> *Keep in mind that you can hear the meter in which a poet has composed a speech or poem even while you can hear how the poet has, at times, varied that meter.*

> ❧ In a Shakespeare play, speeches in **VERSE** are composed with a repeating pattern of stressed and unstressed syllables and are divided into deliberate lines. Shakespeare's verse is composed in meter.

> ❧ In a Shakespeare play, speeches in **PROSE** are composed without a repeating pattern of stressed and unstressed syllables and are not divided into deliberate lines. Prose is not composed in meter.

Examples of VERSE in *Othello*:

> *Desdemona*   So help me every spirit sanctified
> As I have spoken for you all my best,
> And stood within the blank of his displeasure
> For my free speech. You must awhile be patient. (3.4.124-7)
>
> *Brabantio*   So let the Turk of Cyprus us beguile,
> We lose it not so long as we can smile. (1.3.211-12)

> ❧ *Brabantio's speech above, two lines that have the same meter and that rhyme, is called a **COUPLET**.*

- When you are reading Shakespeare's verse, you will see that the first word of each new line of a speech is capitalized whether or not it begins a new sentence.

- Whatever the size of a book's pages, printers retain the lines of a speech in verse. Thus, often you will see empty space between the end of a line and the right margin of your book's page. If a line of verse is longer than what fits on a particular page, then what remains of the verse line usually is indented and printed directly below.

- When you quote verse, you should retain the capital letters and indicate the line breaks with a forward slash, called a *virgule*. Example: When the Duke advises Brabantio not to grieve about his daughter's secret elopement and marriage, Brabantio responds, "So let the Turk of Cyprus us beguile, / We lose it not so long as we can smile" (1.3.211-12).

An example of PROSE in *Othello*:

> *Iago* Virtue? A fig! 'Tis in ourselves that we are thus
> or thus. Our bodies are gardens, to the which our
> wills are gardeners.   (1.3.319-21)

- When you are reading prose, you will see that lines are printed until a word nearly reaches the right margin of the page. The first word of a new line, which varies depending on the size of the book, is not capitalized unless it happens to begin a new sentence.

☙ An **IAMB** is a poetic foot of one unstressed syllable (marked "˘") followed by one stressed syllable (marked "/"). Examples of single words that are iambs are:

$$\breve{\text{con}}\acute{\text{sent}} \qquad \breve{\text{sub}}\acute{\text{due}} \qquad \breve{\text{des}}\acute{\text{pise}}$$

☙ **IAMBIC PENTAMETER** names the meter of a line of verse with five ("penta") iambs. Two examples:

> *Desdemona* Ĭ sáw Ŏthéllŏ's vísăge ín hĭs mínd,   (1.3.253)

> *Desdemona* Sŏme blóodў pássĭon shákes yŏur vérў fráme. (5.2.44)

☙ Marking the stressed and unstressed syllables of a line of verse in the manner above is called **SCANSION**. To **SCAN** a line of verse is to listen for and mark its stressed and unstressed syllables and to notice what kind and how many of the repeating foot make up the line. Scansion also includes noticing any variations in the meter of a line. *(See pages 88-89 for examples of variations in iambic pentameter.)*

Sometimes a line of verse is spoken by more than one character. Here is a single iambic pentameter line shared by Othello and Desdemona:

Othello ˘ / ˘ / ˘ /
I saw the handkerchief.

Desdemona ˘ / ˘ /
He found it then. (5.2.66)

Note that Desdemona's speech is indented to show that it finishes Othello's line.

🙟 A **TROCHEE** is a poetic foot of one stressed syllable followed by one unstressed syllable. Examples of single words that are trochees are:

/ ˘   / ˘   / ˘
honest   witchcraft   Venice

🙟 A **SPONDEE** is a poetic foot of two stressed syllables. Single words that are spondees often are compound words. Examples from *Othello* are:

/ /   / /   / /
wind-shaked   post-haste   light-winged

Much of *Othello* is composed in iambic pentameter, but you will hear many variations in the meter. Below are two to listen for. Consider what a variation calls attention to and what it may add to a speech's meanings.

🙟 Some iambic lines replace one of the iambs with a trochee, a **TROCHEE SUBSTITUTION**.

Here's an example of an iambic pentameter line that begins with a trochee substitution:

Brabantio / ˘ ˘ / ˘ / ˘ / ˘ /
Damned as thou art, thou hast enchanted her, (1.2.62)

And here's an example of a midline trochee substitution:

Othello ˘ / ˘ / / ˘ ˘ / ˘ /
On horror's head horrors accumulate, (3.3.370)

🙞 Some iambic lines end with an extra unstressed syllable. Such a line is said to have a **FEMININE ENDING**. An example:

Brabantio   Ŏ thóu fŏul thíef, whĕre hást thŏu stówed mў dáughtĕr?
(1.2.61)

Scanning a line of poetry requires some interpretation: not every reader will hear a line the same way. Consider Brabantio's above line.

Some readers might hear "O thou foul thief" as two iambs, in which case the line would be scanned:

Ŏ thóu fŏul thíef, whĕre hást thŏu stówed mў dáughtĕr? (1.2.61)

But others might hear "O thou foul thief" as an iamb followed by a spondee in which case it would be scanned:

Ŏ thóu fóul thíef, whĕre hást thŏu stówed mў dáughtĕr? (1.2.61)

🙞 When an iambic line replaces one of the iambs with a spondee—it's called a **SPONDEE SUBSTITUTION**.

Here's a line of Iago's that could be scanned in two ways:

How poor are they that have not patience!   (2.3.346)

To some readers, the line might suggest that the word *patience* is spoken in three syllables, in which case it would be scanned:

Hŏw póor ărе théy thăt háve nŏt pátiĕnce!   (2.3.346)

To other readers, the line might suggest that the final syllable of the final iamb is dropped, in which case it would be scanned:

Hŏw póor ărе théy thăt háve nŏt pátiĕnce!   (2.3.346)

🙞 The meter of an iambic line that lacks the stressed syllable of its final iamb is named CATALECTIC IAMBIC PENTAMETER.

APPENDIX 2. READING FIGURATIVE LANGUAGE—
AN INTRODUCTION TO METAPHOR, SIMILE, METONYMY, & SYNECDOCHE

Shakespeare's plays are famous for their figures of speech, which are rich in meaning and sometimes difficult to understand. What follows is an introduction to four key figures of speech—metaphor, simile, metonymy, and synecdoche—along with some techniques you can use as you work to understand them.

> ✒ A **METAPHOR** asserts that one thing is another thing and demands that we imagine how it can be so.
>
> "A rose is a flower" is not a metaphor. A rose is **LITERALLY** a flower. Anyone could find this out by looking up "rose" in a dictionary.
>
> "Love is a rose" is a metaphor because it demands that we imagine how love is like a rose. A metaphor can be understood as true only if taken **FIGURATIVELY**.

Our English word *metaphor* is borrowed from Greek. "*Meta*" means *trans-* or *across*, and "*phor*" means *port* or *carry*; thus, *metaphor* can be translated as *transport*. The metaphor above transports a *rose* from the world of gardening to explain something in the world of emotions, namely, *love*. Metaphors explain something in one world by transporting something from a distant world for comparison.

One way to analyze a metaphor is to sort its TENOR and VEHICLE, terms coined by I. A. Richards in his 1936 book *The Philosophy of Rhetoric*.

> ✒ The **TENOR** is the subject of the metaphor—what the speaker is talking about.
>
> ✒ The **VEHICLE** is what is transported for comparison to illuminate some quality of the tenor.
>
> In the metaphor "love is a rose," *love* is the tenor and *rose* is the vehicle.

The combination of a metaphor's vehicle and tenor prompts you to recognize that you're hearing or reading a metaphor because the statement would be otherwise absurd or impossible. As Richards emphasizes, the interaction of the tenor and the vehicle produces the metaphor's meaning.

Take, for example, the opening of Shakespeare's Sonnet 68:

> Thus is his cheek the map of days outworn,

When we read this line, we realize that a literal cheek cannot also be a literal map, and so we know that we're reading a metaphor. Here *cheek* is the tenor—what the speaker is talking about—and *map* is the vehicle—what the speaker has transported from the world of diagrams, paper, and ink to describe "cheek" by comparison.

Sometimes it is helpful to sort the metaphor's vehicle and tenor in a chart:

vehicle	:	tenor
map	:	cheek

And sometimes it is helpful to sketch the metaphor, trying to show both its vehicle (cheek) and its tenor (map). Here is an example:

G. Minette

🍂 A **SIMILE** asserts that one thing is "like" or "as" another thing and demands that we imagine how.

"Lucinda is like her grandmother" is not a simile. It is a **LITERAL** statement.

"Lucinda is like a hurricane" is a simile. It is a **FIGURATIVE** statement.

Of course we may have to figure out how Lucinda is like her grandmother, but comparing Lucinda and her grandmother—who both are human, female, and kin—doesn't demand that we use our imagination to find similarities in altogether different categories of things as we must if we are to understand how a human being is like a storm.

Like metaphors, similes work by comparison, but with the word *like* or *as*, similes indicate their comparisons more explicitly. Similes announce the relationship between the tenor and vehicle more formally. Consider, for example, the simile Iago uses to describe a kind of "duteous" servant who, Iago says, "[w]ears out" or spends "his time"

>much like his master's ass,
>For nought but provender [.] (1.1.43-6)

Here, as Iago explains to Roderigo what an overly-duteous servant can expect to receive for his service, he transports a beast of burden—an *ass* or donkey—to describe a servant who will get nothing from his master but enough food to keep him alive and working. (*Nought* means "nothing"; *provender* is "dry food, as hay, oats, etc., for horses or cattle" (*OED* 2).) You could chart the simile:

vehicle	:	tenor
ass	:	servant

The metaphor that opens Sonnet 68 articulates both tenor and vehicle—the cheek and the map—and makes clear their relationship: the cheek "is" the map. Sometimes, however, a metaphor does not name both tenor and vehicle. Or sometimes a metaphor does not state so clearly how the vehicle corresponds to the tenor. Such metaphors require more interpretation.

Consider, for example, Iago's complaint, upon Cassio's having been appointed lieutenant, that he "must be be-lee'd and calmed." Continuing his earlier complaints about Cassio being merely "bookish" and an "arithmetician" with no practical battle experience, Iago refers to Cassio as "debitor and creditor" (a bookkeeper) and "this counter-caster":

> And I, [. . .]
> must be be-lee'd and calmed
> By debitor and creditor, this counter-caster. (1.1.27-9)

First, some definitions:

- *Be-lee'd* means, "To get (a ship) into such a position that the wind is intercepted from her" (*OED* 1).

- *Calmed*, which can mean "Detained by a calm" (*OED* b), refers to a sailboat that cannot move due to lack of wind in its sails.

We know that Iago speaks a metaphor because he has not been becalmed literally: he is not a sailing ship. But Iago doesn't say explicitly what has happened to him.

We can start interpreting the metaphor by charting:

vehicle	:	tenor
be-lee'd	:	?
calmed	:	?

Then, we can make a logical interpretation based on the context of Iago's statement. Sometimes that context suggests more than one interpretation. For instance, we could say:

vehicle	:	tenor
be-lee'd	:	blocked by Cassio from Othello's noticing me for lieutenant
calmed	:	unable to rise in the ranks of the army

Or we could say:

vehicle	:	tenor
be-lee'd	:	blocked by Cassio from Othello's recognition
calmed	:	unable to perform his job (because so disappointed and angry)

Sometimes a statement or speech articulates more than one part of a metaphor's vehicle or tenor. Consider Othello's plan for what he will do if he "proves" Desdemona has been unfaithful:

> Othello   If I do prove her haggard,
>   Though that the jesses were my dear heartstrings,
>   I'd whistle her off, and let her down the wind
>   To prey at fortune.   (3.3.260-3)

Here are four steps that can help lead to an accurate and productive analysis of such a metaphor. I have included sample analysis for each step.

STEP 1. IDENTIFY THE METAPHOR'S SPEAKER, AUDIENCE, & CONTEXT.

Jot down speaker and audience, and briefly review the immediate and relevant context of the speech.

Example:

> Othello to Self or Audience. Iago has just left after suggesting to Othello that his wife, Desdemona, might be deceiving him and that he should observe her with Cassio. Othello is left alone considering the possibility that his wife is unfaithful.

STEP 2. IDENTIFY THE METAPHOR'S VEHICLES.

Underline all the elements of the metaphor's vehicle in the speech.

> *You can find a metaphor's vehicle by looking for the parts that would be absurd if taken literally with the tenor.*
>
> *Be sure to look up unfamiliar words!* **Haggard** *describes a "wild female hawk" that is "untamed" (OED n.2, 1; adj. 1). When training a hawk, a falconer can attach a leash to a* **jess,** *which is a "short strap fastened round each of the legs of a hawk used in falconry" (OED 1a). In Shakesepare's day,* **heartstrings** *were "any cord-like structure attached to or believed to support the heart" (OED 1).*
>
> *Here you can recognize that "haggard" is part of the vehicle because it would be absurd to imagine that Desdemona literally is a hawk with jesses around her legs.*

Example:

>   If I do prove her <u>haggard</u>,
> Though that the <u>jesses</u> were my dear heartstrings,
> I'd <u>whistle</u> her <u>off</u>, and <u>let her down the wind</u>
> To <u>prey</u> at fortune.

STEP 3. SORT THE METAPHOR'S VEHICLE & TENOR.

    A. Start by listing the elements of the vehicle and tenor the speaker states explicitly. Leave blank spaces for the corresponding parts of the vehicle and tenor implied.

Example:

vehicle	:	tenor
?_____	:	I (Othello)
?_____	:	her (my wife Desdemona)
haggard	:	?_____
jesses	:	heartstrings
whistle off	:	?_____
let down the wind	:	?_____
prey	:	?_____
?_____	:	fortune

    B. Then, think about the analogies and fill in those blanks.

You might find it helpful to identify the worlds of the vehicle and the tenor. For instance, the vehicle here is from the world of falconry—of falconers who tame hawks and train them to hunt for them—and the tenor is from the world of marriage.

As you think about the analogies, be sure to review the full list of meanings of any key words.

As you identify missing parts of the vehicle, you might find it helpful to ask yourself questions like, "What literally would a haggard (untamed) hawk do to cause its falconer to let her go?" or "On what would a freed haggard hawk prey?"

As you try to understand the tenor, you might find it helpful to ask yourself questions like: "How could heartstrings be like jesses or leashes?"

Remember that filling in the blanks requires interpretation and that there may be more than one way to interpret accurately.

Example:

vehicle (world of falconry)	:	tenor (world of marriage)
falconer	:	I (Othello)
hawk	:	her (my wife Desdemona)
haggard	:	adulterous
jesses	:	heartstrings
whistle off	:	dismiss, turn out
let down the wind	:	let wherever circumstances move her
prey	:	find her own
on what she finds alone	:	fortune

STEP 4. ARTICULATE THE METAPHOR'S MEANINGS & IMPLICATIONS.

First, think carefully about the metaphor's specific vehicle. In the case of this metaphor, think about the qualities of falconers and hawks and how a falconer tames a hawk so that it hunts but brings the prey to the hunter. Then, think about how the qualities of the vehicle are transported onto the metaphor's tenor.

Keep in mind that not all of the implications and meanings of a metaphor are necessarily intended by the character who speaks the metaphor. Even if a metaphor's implications are not intended by a character, they nonetheless can become meaningful in the play.

Example:

> As Othello considers the action he will take if he proves his wife unfaithful, he imagines the potentially adulterous Desdemona as "haggard," a term that figures Othello as a falconer and his wife as his inadequately tamed hawk. Since a falconer profits when a tamed hawk pursues and seizes its prey and returns the prey to him, the metaphor implies that a husband will receive valuable things from a chaste or "tamed" wife. If a falconer's hawk must be desirous enough to hunt for prey but tame enough to accept the falconer's reward in exchange for it, the metaphor further implies that a wife should have desires but that those desires should benefit and be controlled by her husband. A hawk naturally has the power and skill to hunt and catch prey that a falconer could never obtain by himself; thus, the metaphor implies that a wife is naturally powerful enough to get things for her husband that he could never get on his own. Othello's metaphor transforms the figurative bond of marriage into the literally binding jesses, the leather bands fastened to a hawk's legs to which a falconer's leash could be attached. Depicting those bonds as his heartstrings, Othello reveals that he is prepared to cut out a vital part of himself to be rid of an adulterous wife. Thus, Othello's metaphor implies that he will be gravely injured if he "whistles off" his wife.

Whereas metaphor and simile work by comparison, metonymy and synecdoche work by association or scale.

> One thing standing for another associated thing is called **METONYMY**.

Iago uses metonymy when he decides "to abuse Othello's ear / That [Cassio] is too familiar with his wife" (1.3.389-90). An *ear* is associated with hearing, so "Othello's ear" stands here for Othello's capacity to hear and understand.

Iago also uses metonymy when he later claims, "For I fear Cassio with my night-cap too" (2.1.296). Iago's fear that Cassio has worn his *night-cap* stands in for his fear that Cassio has taken his place in his bed, sleeping with his wife.

> Part of a thing standing for the whole thing is called **SYNECDOCHE**.

Roderigo speaks a synecdoche when he exclaims about Othello: "What a full fortune does the thick lips owe, / If he can carry't thus!" (1.1.64-5). Roderigo thus calls the man Othello by one facial feature, "thick lips."

The difference between *being associated with* and *being part of* can be very slim, so it can be difficult to decide whether to classify a figure of speech as metonymy or synecdoche. The difference between metonymy and metaphor, however, is larger and more significant. In order to understand a metaphor or simile we need to imagine how a tenor in one world compares to a vehicle from a distant world: we need to imagine how one thing *is* or *is like* another thing with which it ordinarily is not associated. Unlike metaphor and simile, metonymy and synecdoche are from the same world as the things they stand for.

APPENDIX 3. ON HOW AN EDITION OF *OTHELLO* IS MADE

Anyone who publishes a Shakespeare play has made a number of decisions about how to transform the earliest surviving copies of the play into a current edition. As you develop your own interpretation of *Othello*, it is helpful to be aware of what role an editor has played in making the edition of the play you are reading.

None of Shakespeare's handwritten play manuscripts has survived, and as far as anyone knows, Shakespeare was not involved in the publication of his plays. Scholars cannot be certain about when Shakespeare wrote *Othello*. There is a record of a court performance of the play in 1604, and scholars date the play's writing as sometime between 1601 and 1604. While Shakespeare was alive, some of his individual plays were published in small books called *quartos*; however, there is no existing edition of *Othello* published before Shakespeare died in 1616. A quarto of *Othello* was published in 1622 (now called the *First Quarto* or *Q1*), and *Othello* was included in a collection of Shakespeare's plays, entitled *Mr. William Shakespeares Comedies, Histories, & Tragedies*. This large book, called a *folio*, was first published in 1623. (Scholars now refer to this first edition of Shakespeare's collected plays as the *First Folio* or *F1*.)

Here are the opening lines of the play as they appear in the surviving First Quarto and First Folio:

The 1622 Quarto

The 1623 Folio

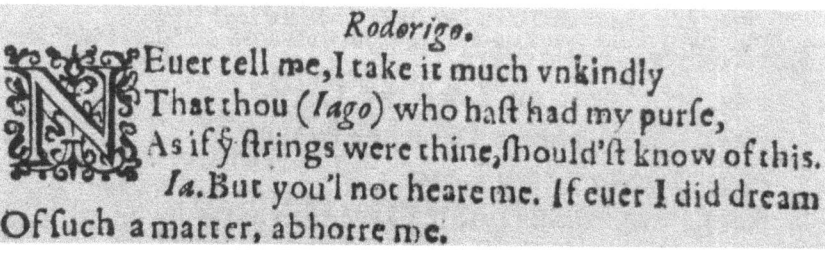

And here it is as printed in the 2005 Yale University Press edition of the play (1.1.1-5):

>   *Roderigo*   Never tell me, I take it much unkindly
>   That thou, Iago, who has had my purse
>   As if the strings were thine, shouldst know of this.
>   *Iago*   But you will not hear me. If ever I did dream
>   Of such a matter, abhor me.

There are a number of differences between the early quartos and folio and any modern edition of *Othello*:

- **Editors standardize spelling and punctuation according to current practices.** So, for instance, the First Quarto's "heare" is now printed as "hear." (You also will notice that "should'st" is spelled with a "long s," a letter no longer available among English fonts.)

98

- **Editors add stage directions not in the Quartos or First Folio.** Often editors distinguish their own stage directions from those in the Quartos or First Folio by enclosing them in parentheses or brackets. When, in act 3, scene 3, Emilia tells Iago that she has Desdemona's handkerchief, the Yale edition prints the stage direction *"snatches it"* (3.3.315). However, neither the early quarto or the folio includes a stage direction. Editors base such stage directions on their reading of the play, so you should always test them by reading the lines closely and considering other possible stagings. *(See question 18c on page 29 and question 44 on page 54 for exercises on reading an editor's stage directions critically.)*

- **Editors mark act, scene, and line numbers.** The First Quarto does not mark sections of the play with act, scene, or line numbers; the First Folio does not mark line numbers. Editors usually adopt the act and scene numbers marked in the First Folio, to which they add line numbers. Because some speeches in the play are in prose, not verse, a modern edition's line numbers vary depending on the size of the page. *(For explanations of verse and prose, see appendix 1, pages 86-87.)*

- **Editors include notes that explain selected words and phrases.** In some notes editors provide definitions for words that might be unfamiliar to us now or whose meanings were different in Shakespeare's day. For instance, editors often note that the word *extravagant* in Roderigo's description of Othello as "an extravagant and wheeling stranger" (1.1.134-5) means "roaming" or "vagrant" (*OED* 1)—not "exceeding the bounds of economy" or "wasteful" (*OED* 7) as it more often does now. Editors do not list all possible definitions of words they gloss, but you can check the *Oxford English Dictionary* for a complete list of seventeenth-century meanings of any word. In other notes editors may offer more extensive explanations of the meaning of a phrase or a line. Read such notes critically: there may be additional ways to understand the phrase or line.

Most modern editions of *Othello* are derived from some combination of the 1622 Quarto and the 1623 Folio. Some basic information about each:

The 1622 Quarto. The title page of this earliest existing quarto reads: "The Tragœdy of Othello, The Moore of Venice. As it hath beene diuerse times acted at the Globe, and at the Black-Friers, by his Maiesties Seruants." (The letters "u" and "v" were interchangeable in Shakespeare's day!)

The 1623 Folio. Seven years after Shakespeare's death, two of his fellow actors, John Heminges and Henry Condell, collected and edited the thirty-six plays of the First Folio. Its title page advertises that it contains the plays "Published according to the True Originall Copies." None of Shakespeare's handwritten play manuscripts—no "true" or "original" copy—has survived. Moreover, as a playwright who was part-owner of a theater company, Shakespeare very well have may revised his plays during the course of their various performances or adapted them for particular occasions, further complicating the idea of an "original" or "perfect" copy. (*Perfect* can mean *complete*.) If, as most scholars believe, Shakespeare himself was not involved in the publication of his plays, then he did not make any choices about their publication.

Editors have to make choices when confronted with the many differences in these two early texts. As you can see in the opening lines, the 1622 Quarto contains profanity deleted from the 1623 Folio. ("Tush" was slang for *backside* and "S'blood" a contraction of *God's blood*.) These, and many other such deletions, were likely a result of government censoring before the publication of the 1623 Folio. Another notable difference is in Othello's final speech: in the First Folio's act 5, scene 2, Othello compares himself to "the base Judean" whereas in the first quarto he compares himself to "the base Indian" (5.2.346). If you become interested in such differences, you can compare your edition of *Othello* to the early texts by finding facsimiles of them in your library or on the Internet.[2]

---

[2] Such websites include *The Shakespeare Quarto Archives* (at http://www.quartos.org/index.html) and *Internet Shakespeare Editions* (at http://internetshakespeare.uvic.ca/Library/facsimile/).

ACKNOWLEDGMENTS

Over the years I have had the pleasure of reading Shakespeare's plays with hundreds of students at Friends Seminary. Their enthusiastic interest in the plays, their willingness to work to understand them, and their fresh interpretations first inspired me to develop and publish guides to the plays. Exchanges with colleagues and students at other schools have encouraged me to continue the series.

I continue to be thankful for Lauren Simkin Berke's imaginative reading and exceptional craft in cover illustration and design. I am grateful to Robert Lauder, Principal of Friends Seminary, for his ongoing support and to my colleagues for their enduring camaraderie and help. Heather Cross convinced me to make the guides available to the general public, made key suggestions about their structure, and responded generously to many questions. Chris Doire, Josh Goren, Philip Kay, Cara Murray, Thomas O'Connell, Katherine Olson, and Craig Saslow offered valuable comments as I developed the guides' preface and appendices. Tommy Fagin's careful review saved me from several errors.

I am grateful to Donna Anstey at Yale University Press for permission to include the image of the lines scanned from the 1954 Yale University Press facsimile edition of *Mr. William Shakespeares Comedies, Histories, & Tragedies* and to Michael J. B. Allen for permission to include the image of the 1622 Quarto lines scanned from the University of California Press's 1981 facsimile edition, *Shakespeare's Plays in Quarto*, edited by Michael Allen and Kenneth Muir.

My understanding of *Othello* has developed over years of conversations with Sarah Spieldenner, and I am thankful, most recently, for her perceptive, meticulous comments on this guide. I am once again grateful to Patrick Morrissey for his vital suggestions about the appendices, his discerning comments on the questions, and his careful editing of the manuscript. Final thanks are to Gordon Minette for help with matters large and small as I prepared *A Guide to Reading Shakespeare's Othello* for publication.

www.ingramcontent.com/pod-product-compliance
Lightning Source LLC
Chambersburg PA
CBHW080445110426
42743CB00016B/3285